CATULLUS

A LEGAMUS
TRANSITIONAL READER

THE LEGAMUS READER SERIES

edited by
Kenneth F. Kitchell Jr., University of Massachusetts Amherst,
and Thomas J. Sienkewicz, Monmouth College

The *LEGAMUS* series was created to address the needs of today's students as they move from "made up" Latin to the Latin of real authors who lived over two thousand years ago. Both established and innovative pedagogical techniques are employed to ease the problems facing students as they begin to read authentic Latin authors. At its core, the series intends to facilitate reading before all else, and the many innovations in the series all stem from a single question: "What makes reading this author difficult for students?"

The series is intended for use in intermediate and upper-level Latin courses in both college and high school. Volumes in the series may be used individually as an introduction to a given author or together to form an upper-division reading course.

Vergil: A LEGAMUS Transitional Reader
THOMAS J. SIENKEWICZ & LEAANN A. OSBURN

Vergil: A LEGAMUS Transitional Reader: Teacher's Guide
LEAANN A. OSBURN & KAREN LEE SINGH

Catullus: A LEGAMUS Transitional Reader
KENNETH F. KITCHELL JR. & SEAN SMITH

Catullus: A LEGAMUS Transitional Reader: Teacher's Guide
SEAN SMITH

Ovid: A LEGAMUS Transitional Reader
CAROLINE PERKINS & DENISE DAVIS-HENRY

Ovid: A LEGAMUS Transitional Reader: Teacher's Guide
CAROLINE PERKINS & DENISE DAVIS-HENRY

Horace: A LEGAMUS Transitional Reader
RONNIE ANCONA & DAVID J. MURPHY

Horace: A LEGAMUS Transitional Reader: Teacher's Guide
DAVID J. MURPHY

Cicero: A LEGAMUS Transitional Reader
JUDITH SEBESTA & MARK HAYNES

Cicero: A LEGAMUS Transitional Reader: Teacher's Guide
JUDITH SEBESTA & MARK HAYNES

Caesar: A LEGAMUS Transitional Reader
ROSE WILLIAMS & HANS-FRIEDRICH MUELLER

Caesar: A LEGAMUS Transitional Reader: Teacher's Guide
ROSE WILLIAMS & HANS-FRIEDRICH MUELLER

CATULLUS
A LEGAMUS
TRANSITIONAL READER

KENNETH F. KITCHELL JR.
& SEAN SMITH

Bolchazy-Carducci Publishers, Inc.
Mundelein, Illinois USA

Series Coeditors: Kenneth F. Kitchell and Thomas J. Sienkewicz

General Editors: Marie Carducci Bolchazy, Laurie Haight Keenan

Contributing Editors: Andrew J. Adams, LeaAnn A. Osburn

Cover Design & Typography: Adam Phillip Velez

Cover Illustration: Auguste Rodin (1840–1917), Eternal Springtime (detail). 1884.
   Timothy McCarthy/Art Resource, NY

Cartography: The Ohio University Cartography Center

LEGAMUS Transitional Reader Series
Catullus: A LEGAMUS Transitional Reader

Kenneth F. Kitchell Jr. and Sean Smith

Bolchazy-Carducci Publishers, Inc.
1570 Baskin Road
Mundelein, Illinois 60060
www.bolchazy.com

Printed in the United States of America
2019
by Kingery Printing

ISBN 978-0-86516-634-9

Library of Congress Cataloging-in-Publication Data

Kitchell, Kenneth Francis, 1947-
  Catullus : a Legamus transitional reader / Kenneth F. Kitchell, Jr. & Sean Smith.
    p. cm. -- (Legamus transitional reader series)
  English; selected texts in Latin.
  ISBN-13: 978-0-86516-634-9 (pbk. : alk. paper)
  ISBN-10: 0-86516-634-X (pbk. : alk. paper)
  1. Latin language--Readers--Poetry. 2. Love poetry, Latin. I. Smith, Sean, 1961- II. Catullus, Gaius Valerius. Selections. 2006 III. Title. IV. Series.

PA2099.C35 2006
478.6'421--dc22

                                                                    2006017356

CONTENTS

LIST OF ILLUSTRATIONS

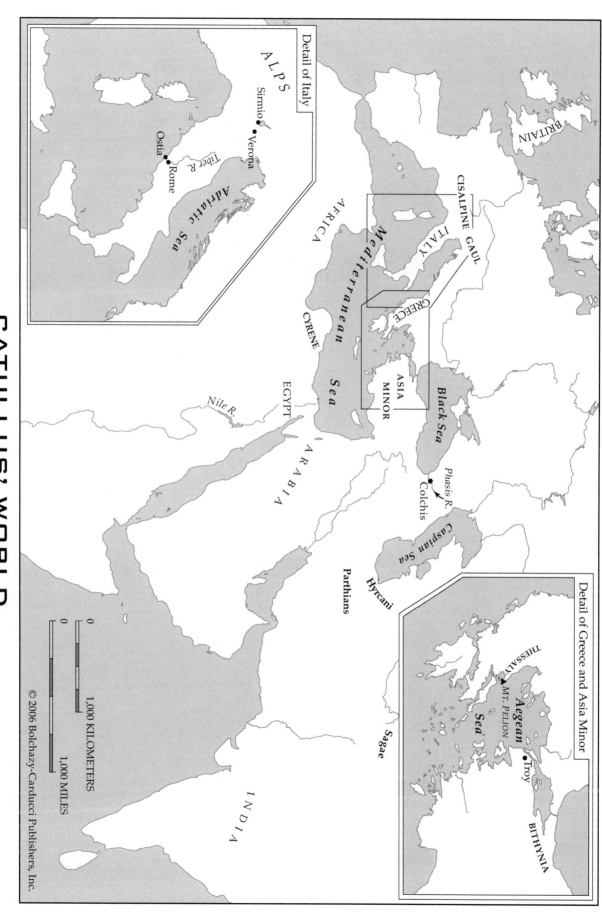

CATULLUS' WORLD

Detail of Italy

ALPS

Sirmio

Verona

Ostia

Rome

Tiber R.

Adriatic Sea

Detail of Greece and Asia Minor

THESSALY

MT. PELION

Aegean Sea

Troy

BITHYNIA

Sagae

Parthians

Hyrcani

Caspian Sea

Colchis

Phasis R.

Black Sea

ASIA MINOR

GREECE

ITALY

CISALPINE GAUL

BRITAIN

Mediterranean Sea

AFRICA

CYRENE

EGYPT

Nile R.

ARABIA

INDIA

0   1,000 KILOMETERS

0   1,000 MILES

© 2006 Bolchazy-Carducci Publishers, Inc.

FOREWORD

THE LEGAMUS TRANSITIONAL READER SERIES

The transition from the "made-up Latin" of today's popular Latin textbooks for first- and second-year Latin students to the "real" Latin of ancient authors represents one of the major hurdles facing today's Latin students and one of the greatest challenges facing us as teachers. In fact, somewhere during the early stages of a student's first encounter with "real" Latin, the student comes to realize that he or she cannot translate upper division authors with anything resembling fluency. While the frustration of the teacher is great, that of the student is even greater and it is little wonder that in most schools the drop-off in enrollment between Latin II and Latin III is astronomical.

The Legamus Committee, sponsored by Bolchazy-Carducci Publishers, was created to study this problem. From its inception, the committee included both college/university and high-school Latin teachers and studied the many problems related to this transition for several years. Members of the committee presented panels and obtained teacher feedback at ACL and CAMWS meetings alike where suggestions from teachers in the audience did much to help us form our plans.

Briefly put, the committee's studies have made clear the following facts. First, to move from the controlled world of an elementary Latin program to the unpredictable world of an actual author is to take a quantum leap that is unparalleled in the students' experience and demands a much wider set of skills than is generally recognized. Students must move from a world of controlled plot line, familiar and recurring characters, repetitive vocabulary, and fairly straightforward word order into a realm where the author does exactly what he wants and does so in elevated language and, often enough, meter. Add expanded vocabulary, rhetorical word order, stylistic quirks of various authors, and the issue of cultural literacy and it is little wonder that modern students often quickly become frustrated in upper division Latin.

Yet, whereas the new generation of elementary textbooks changed radically over the past two to three decades, textbooks which make the transition into reading "real" Latin have lagged behind. They rarely go beyond the now common strategy of having notes and vocabulary on the same page or facing the text (a "trick" as old as the age of manuscripts).

Ironically, this transition was less of a problem before the field changed. It was formerly a universal that after a year of grammar all students would move on to Caesar. Thus, several excellent transitional books were created which gradually and effectively introduced the student to Caesar's vocabulary, style, and syntax. *Fabulae Faciles* is but one example. Today, however, since the upper division curricula are quite varied, a new set of transitional readers is required.

This volume is one in a series of *LEGAMUS* transitional Latin readers designed to facilitate the transition from beginning Latin to reading a major Latin author. Each volume concentrates on the specific problems faced by beginning readers of that particular author. The peculiarities of a Ciceronian sentence, for example, need not be taught in a Vergil transitional reader and teaching the vocabulary of love poetry would be pointless in a Cicero text.

We stress that the series is not intended to produce just another annotated edition of the author. It is not an exhaustive teaching edition of the author. Instead, its purpose is expressly and solely to address those very things which make the transition to reading a given author difficult. Other issues, for example literary interpretation or the niceties of scansion, can wait for the actual course in an author—once the student can actually read that author! The premise is as simple as it is important— identify the specific hurdles students must clear to be able to read a given author and then teach them skills to address each issue.

Here, then, is an overview of the series:

1. Each volume is designed to be used at the point of transition from elementary texts to advanced texts, i.e., at the point when students move from learning grammar and reading made-up texts to reading authentic Latin.

2. The goal of each volume is to enable students to read the unchanged text of that author in as short a time as possible.

3. Volumes are designed to be flexible and to fit into a variety of curricula at both the high school and college levels. They can thus be used individually as an introduction to a particular author but can also be used together in any combination to serve as the textbooks of a survey course.

Each volume is coauthored by a college teacher and a pre-collegiate teacher. Each volume is short, containing a limited number of readings, each one envisioned as a single night's assignment. Passages gradually increase in length and difficulty throughout the volume and gradually introduce the student to quirks of the author's style, vocabulary, grammatical preferences, diction, and the like.

Each reader uses a set tool kit of techniques designed for teaching the student how to read the given author. These include the following:

1. Pre-reading exercises in English or Latin help the student deal with the issue of culturally based impediments to understanding, addressing what E. D. Hirsch has called "cultural literacy." We would hope that the student can thus begin to read each passage, predisposed to understand its contents and thus ready to concentrate solely on the language-based hurdles it presents.

2. Frequently, before the student reads an unchanged passage, she or he is presented with a simplified, rearranged or shortened Latin version of complex passages. Selections of poetry are often given first in a prose summary.

3. The Latin text of complex passages is, at first, often shown in innovative layout and with typography to enable students to see the individual sense units in complex sentences. Such techniques will be used liberally early on, but in every case the rearranged Latin version will be followed directly by the unchanged Latin text of the original. Moreover, the last section of each volume presents unchanged text only. By this time the student, one hopes, will have become accustomed to the author's style.

4. There is frequent use of exercises designed to teach the author's favorite vocabulary and syntax.

5. Other exercises teach major stylistic preferences of the author.

6. Of course, traditional notes and vocabulary will accompany each passage, and a brief grammar and full vocabulary are at the end of each volume.

To move into the world of "real" Latin really means to move into the world of high literature. Imagine having to read Dickens after two years of high school English! It is the hope of the authors and editors that this series will help ease this difficult transition and bring more students into direct contact with the beauty and inspiration reading these authors can provide.

KENNETH F. KITCHELL JR.
University of Massachusetts Amherst

PREFACE

How to Use This Reader

This reader is designed first to help students make the transition from studying Latin grammar and reading "made-up Latin" to reading an authentic ancient text. The book equally will help more experienced students begin to read the poetry of Catullus by highlighting and gradually introducing the poet's more difficult elements of subject matter, vocabulary, syntax and, most importantly, poetic diction and style. It is the aim of the reader to use a variety of devices to introduce these elements to the student and then, gradually, to move the student to reading the unchanged text of Catullus himself.

The poems in the Catullan collection deal with several major themes and the poems do not appear in any particular order. The authors of this reader have chosen to concentrate on three major aspects of Catullus' poetry—his love affair with Lesbia, his friends in the world of Roman poetry, and his longer poems. The reader contains eighteen poems. Sixteen are printed in their entirety and two are selections from longer poems. As the reader's intent is to provide more help for the student at the beginning and then move toward reading the poetry unchanged, the reader should be read in order. To eliminate Catullus' long poems would be to ignore an important aspect of this poet. Yet these poems are rather more difficult than the shorter poems. To help with this fact, the authors have put selections from the longer poems at the end of the current volume. This is not to indicate that these selections are optional—to know Catullus is to know not only his short, impassioned poems "from the heart," but also his longer, Alexandrian poems "from the head." Rather, it was felt that these poems, with their complex language, would be best studied after the difficulties of poetic diction and word order had been first met in the shorter poems.

Teachers might use this book in a variety of ways. As the Foreword explains, these readers are not designed to be intensive studies of any one author, but rather to serve as a practical way to introduce students to an author. As such, this book could effectively be used in the last month of an academic year or semester prior to commencing a longer study of Catullus. Likewise, it could be read in a given semester prior to studying Catullus in depth. The reader could also be paired with other readers from the LEGAMUS series to offer a survey course of Latin authors, with each book providing a careful introduction to the difficulties inherent in reading that author.

The overall, guiding principle of this book, and of the series as a whole, is to enable the student to **read** the words of a given author as quickly as possible. Thus, there is limited mention in this volume of meter (so much more complex in Catullus than in Vergil). Likewise, figures of speech are only mentioned and studied to the extent that they enable the student reader to decipher a complex line of poetry. That is, recognizing **chiasmus** is viewed primarily as a skill necessary for reading comprehension (untangling word order) rather than for admiring poetic craft. Yet to study a poet of this much talent without studying his craft would be senseless and this too receives its attention.

The following paragraphs describe the various parts of the reader designed to help the student read Catullus' unchanged text.

BEFORE YOU READ WHAT CATULLUS WROTE

Many things can make a passage of Latin poetry difficult to understand. One is "context." In this section, therefore, we offer the student enough context to understand what the poem she or he is about to read is going to say. Sometimes this takes the form of explaining the situation at hand (an invitation to a dinner party, the fact that Catullus' lover was a prominent married woman about Rome) and at other times it attempts to put the reader in the proper emotional frame of mind (death of a family member, friendship or love betrayed). Before reading a given passage, some grammar is generally reviewed ("Keep This Grammar in Mind"). This grammar is chosen because it is particularly important for the poem itself or because it is commonly found in Catullus. Do not skip these sections! They will help you read Catullus much more quickly. Indeed, whenever possible, the grammar examples are taken from Catullus' own poems, even ones not included in this volume.

HELPING YOU TO READ WHAT CATULLUS WROTE

In this section, the passage is presented to the reader with a variety of reading aids. Given the book's goals, these are more frequent early on than later. They include:

a. **Vocabulary** English meanings for all the Latin words in this book are to found either in the pull-out vocabulary at the end of the book or within sight of the passage being read. The words in the pull-out represent words that are either very basic to Latin or which appear frequently in Catullus. The running vocabulary attempts not to give all meanings of a word, but meanings best fitting the current context.

b. **Notes** The notes appear on the page facing the passage and are designed first to help the reader understand the passage, and second to introduce the reader to various aspects of Catullan usage. It is our custom to give an answer once or twice but then to expect that this little snippet of information has been learned. We therefore will sometimes refer a student back to a previous spot. Likewise, some notes consist of questions designed to lead the student to an answer rather than merely giving an answer. This is done to prevent the notes from becoming a "hyperlink" to the right answer rather than a way of learning the essentials of Catullan style and diction.

c. **Visual Aids** Poetic word order can be terribly confusing at first. Thus, rewritten versions of the poems are often presented in a section called "Making Sense of It." These versions often simplify the word order and supply in parentheses words that are routinely left out in Latin (a process called "gapping"). Special fonts are frequently used to show which words should be taken together, such as noun-adjective agreements. These aids are gradually reduced until, at the end of the first portion of the book, the student is reading unchanged Catullan poems. The use of special fonts is discontinued after Poem 83 until the end of Section I. In Section II font help is used for both poems and a rewrite is used for the first selection only. Macrons are used throughout the text.

WHAT CATULLUS ACTUALLY WROTE

In this section the same poem is presented, but without any rewriting or gapping aids supplied. Initially, fonts are still used to help the reader become accustomed to Catullan word order and poetic diction. Since the bulk of notes and vocabulary have already been given in the "Making Sense of It" passage, the students will find that they need very few aids to read this version of the poem—in fact, the poet's own words.

AFTER READING WHAT CATULLUS WROTE

Once the student has understood what the poem says, it is time to study *how* the poet said it and what it all means. Thus, this section contains diverse items. In "Thinking about How the Author Writes," readers will be asked to think about such things as vocabulary choice, and to concentrate of some major Catullan grammar points. In "Thinking about What You Read" the readers are challenged to interact with the poem on a variety of levels ranging from sharing the poet's own emotions and feelings to analyzing how Catullus put together a poem for maximum impact. Occasionally this section will also contain some exercises on Catullan vocabulary, teaching the vocabulary of love and poetry.

GRAMMATICAL APPENDIX

Following the last reading passage are Appendices that contain information for quick reference. The first, the Grammatical Appendix, is adapted from *Graphic Latin Grammar,* a summary of the grammatical forms and syntax of Latin grammar. This Appendix is included to provide students with an at-hand concise reference should they need it. Such a reference has the advantage of giving a great deal of information in a highly concentrated form, so that students will not need to look far to find the paradigm or explanation they need. *Graphic Latin Grammar* is copyright © Bolchazy-Carducci Publishers, Inc., and this adaptation of it is included here with the publisher's permission.

ACKNOWLEDGEMENTS

Our thanks first to Bolchazy-Carducci Publishers whose foresight and concern for the field of Classics helped found the *LEGAMUS* series. Equally, the sound advice and pedagogical instincts of coeditor Thomas Sienkewicz are to be found on every page. Thanks also to Gary Varney, who proofread the manuscript and saved us from many typographical errors. Our deep thanks to the many teachers who helped for the series in general and this book in particular through their thoughtful comments at various presentations throughout the country as the series in general and this book in particular came into being.

The teachers and students who field-tested preliminary versions of the text gave generously of their time and insights and contributed to the book in more ways than they will ever know:

Nicole Brown	Hudson High School
Sharyn Davis	Chelmsford High School
Patricia Jacquart	Scituate High School
John Oksanish	Walpole High School
C. Emil Penarubia	Boston College High School
Roger Stone	Austin Preparatory School
Sally Teague	Holyoke Catholic High School

We must not fail to mention our own students who have enlightened us throughout our teaching careers. It is from them—from their simultaneous joy at and frustration with reading Catullus and other authors—that the nucleus for this book and series arose. Finally, of course, to our families and wives, for constant support and encouragement.

AN INTRODUCTION TO CATULLUS

THE *LIBELLUS* THAT ALMOST WASN'T

We came very close to having nothing left of Catullus other than his name and some references to him in other authors. He lived a short and emotion-packed life filled with good friends and passionate love relationships and was part of one of the greatest revolutions in poetry writing the world has seen. Later Roman poets mention him with fond praise. Yet, if not for some extraordinary luck, we would never have had a chance to read his glorious poetry ourselves.

Catullus was one of the most widely read poets in ancient Rome at the time of Caesar, Pompey, and Cicero. We know from the first poem that Catullus presented an early copy of his poems to his friend and fellow poet Cornelius. We know too that an ancient book was "published" by being copied by hand in copy shops (*scriptoria*) throughout the city. There must have been hundreds, if not thousands of copies at one time. We can imagine that most noble families in Rome and outlying cities had to have a copy of this newest of Roman poets.

But over time, the number diminished. The books were written on papyrus and after a while papyrus becomes brittle and crumbles away. Eventually parchment (*vellum*) replaced papyrus and gradually copies of disintegrating papyrus rolls were transferred to vellum. But, as one might expect, only the works that were popular in that day and age were copied frequently, and during the early Middle Ages Catullus was not terribly popular. Surely his open talk of love and sexuality, coupled with his penchant for strong language, kept him off most monastery bookshelves and it was here that most copying was done.

For a long period of time in the Middle Ages, then, no one even read Catullus' poetry, because all copies of the text had been lost. In about the year 1300 someone in Verona found a scroll at the bottom of a basket with 116 poems in it. This was the bulk of Catullus' *libellus!*

The bad news is that this scroll, called V for "Verona," disappeared soon after. The good news is that two copies had been made, neither any earlier than 1375 AD. One of these, called O, is now at Oxford. The other, called X by most scholars, may have been owned by the Italian poet Petrarch. It has also disappeared, but we have two copies of it, G and R. The chart on page xxii shows this family tree.

After this fourteenth-century rediscovery, Catullus became as popular again among Renaissance love poets as he had been among ancient writers and his poetry is widely read, admired, and imitated even today. One final poem, a marriage hymn, was found in Paris in a ninth-century manuscript called T. This poem, number 62 (not in this collection), was not in the manuscripts descended from V so its existence is due solely to this ninth-century anthology and is the earliest copy of a Catullan poem we own.

Many copies of these main manuscripts exist, each with its own errors and variable readings. Thomson (1978, ix) estimates that there are about 150 manuscripts to deal with in all. But they are all copies derived from O, G, R, or T.

As you use this book, and as you learn to read the words of one of the greatest poets ever to live, stop and consider now and then that almost all our knowledge of his poetry is based on a single scroll carelessly tossed in a basket and the good taste of an unknown anthologist who lived in the ninth century.

THE MANUSCRIPTS OF CATULLUS

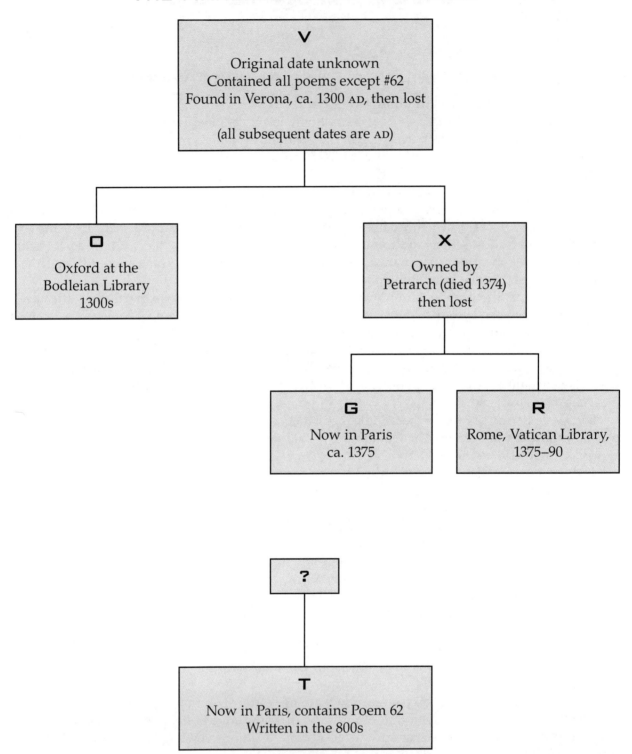

Fig. 1.
The Manuscripts of Catullus

CATULLUS' LIFE AND TIMES

We know precious little about Catullus outside of what he tells us in his poetry. His name was probably *Gaius Valerius Catullus*. The *praenomen* "Quintus" appears in a few places but scholars believe it is incorrect. He was born in the northern city of Verona (see map, p. xi) where his father must have been wealthy enough to provide his son with an excellent education, and family wealth probably purchased the villa in Sirmio that Catullus dearly loved. We know from his poetry that his friends in Rome all came from the best of families, and family connections probably helped Catullus' brother secure a governmental post in the province of Bithynia, where he died. Catullus himself spent some time in Asia Minor, serving with the governor of Bithynia, one Gaius Memmius. It was not a great post for Catullus and he attacks Memmius brutally in his poems. Almost everything else about his life is the result of clever guesswork.

When did he live? The earliest person to assign him dates was St. Jerome (348–420 AD). Jerome gives dates of 87–57 BC and tells us Catullus died in his thirtieth year of life. But Catullus mentions Pompey's second consulship (54 BC) and since no poem can be dated after this year, it is commonly taken that he died in 54 BC. If we keep Jerome's statement about Catullus' lifespan (and Jerome had access to better records than we do) then a birth date of 84 BC is logical.

For what follows we will use the dates of 84–54 BC for Catullus' life. What sort of world did he know? Horace was about ten years old when Catullus died and Vergil was 15. Ovid was born about 12 years after Catullus' death. The golden age of poetry was yet to come, therefore. The great historian Livy was still a child when Catullus died.

But Catullus did know some greats. At Rome he almost surely knew the historians Sallust and Nepos, and the philosopher/poet Lucretius died at about the same time Catullus did. More tellingly, Catullus knew Julius Caesar well enough to get into some sort of spat with him (the reconciliation is mentioned in one of Catullus' poems), and he and Cicero were contemporaries, although Cicero was decidedly older.

We do not know exactly when he came to live in Rome, but whether he was in Verona or Rome, he surely lived in interesting times. Catullus was a child when Spartacus led a revolt of slaves and gladiators throughout Italy (73 BC). He saw the rise of the first triumvirate with Caesar, Pompey and Crassus, and read the dispatches sent back from Gaul by Caesar. He is an exact contemporary to the plot of Catiline to overthrow the government and probably followed the speeches of Cicero closely.

In short, Catullus lived in momentous times. The power plays between members of the first triumvirate would soon spill over into full civil war and blood would run in the streets of Rome. But in his time things in Rome must have been relatively calm. The poems we have show us a life in which there was ample scope for a poet to meet with his friends at parties or to idle in the forum displaying his latest girlfriend. There were entire days spent in discussing and writing poetry with one's friends, and, of course, there was time for love.

LESBIA

Although Catullus wrote many sorts of poetry (more on this below) he always has, and always will, be best known for his love affair with a married woman he calls "Lesbia." She was not his only lover to be sure, but beyond question she evoked the greatest passion in him.

Lesbia is a pseudonym, as was customary in Roman love poetry. It is almost certain that her real name was Clodia and that she was married to Quintus Caecilius Metellus Celer and was the sister of Publius Clodius Pulcher.

The mere names seem lifeless, but the Clodii were anything but dull. The husband was an important public figure, serving as governor of Cisalpine Gaul. While he was gone rumors about his wife's behavior ran rampant in Rome. After he returned home he served as consul in 60 BC, only to die the next year. There is no doubt that his wife continued to engage in affairs until he died. One poem of Catullus even tells us that the three met face-to-face when Catullus and "Lesbia" were engaged in their affair, but that the husband was ignorant of the whole thing.

Clodia's brother, Publius, was one of the most notorious young men in all of Rome. He was active in the politics of the day, mostly being remembered as causing trouble, and was central to a major scandal that rocked Rome in 62/1 BC, when Catullus was about 23. Clodius had put on women's clothing in order to sneak into the ceremonies honoring the "Bona Dea," "Good Goddess." This was impiety of the highest order, and none other than Cicero himself prosecuted Clodius. In the process Cicero savaged the behavior of the Clodii as a whole and gave a scathing picture of Clodia in the process. Clodius only escaped being convicted with the help of Crassus, who bribed the jury. Clodius got some revenge, for as tribune in 58 BC he helped engineer Cicero's exile.

Clodia herself seems to have been beautiful to be sure, but also intelligent and inclined to appreciate poetry. Her morality is surely questionable, and she treated her succession of lovers abominably. But there was more to her than this. Catullus' name for her, "Lesbia," is a reference to Sappho, the most famous female writer from Greek antiquity. Sappho was born on Lesbos ca. 612 BC and her poetry is still moving today. The poem in which Catullus describes how he first saw Clodia is, in fact, largely an translation of a Sapphic ode. You will read this poem below. As a Roman Sappho, Lesbia inspired both love and poetry in Catullus and the result is his legacy to us.

CATULLUS' POETRY

The collection

Scholars have expended enormous amounts of ingenuity and energy trying to resolve how our poems came to exist in the form they do. Are they what Catullus actually published? Almost certainly not. They probably represent an anthology of his works, and many poems may have been lost to us. Consider Poem 62, for example, which only appeared in one manuscript.

We are not even sure of how many poems we have. Most editions show 116 poems, but poems 17–19 are not in the manuscripts; they were added by a scholar in 1554. Whether they are legitimate candidates is debatable. Other poems (e.g. 2, 14, 95) are sometimes broken into two pieces by some editors.

Despite all this, some major groupings are fairly obvious.

Group I (poems 1–60). These poems are called the "polymetrics" because Catullus is at great pains to show his ability to write verse in a wide variety of meters. These deal with Lesbia, other loves, friendship, social norms, satire, and Catullus' social life.

Group II (poems 61–68). These are the "long poems," cleverly named because they are, in fact, long—or at least longer than normal. The longest has only 408 lines.

Group III (poems 69–116). This group is again short and all the poems are written in elegiac meter. The subject matter is once more quite varied and some of Catullus' fiercest attacks on others appear in this section.

Catullus definitely did not publish the poems in this order. For one thing, in Poem 1 he refers to his work as slender. All these poems would produce a decidedly un-slender roll of papyrus. And Poem 14b, a fragment, also looks like a introduction. Was this for a second volume? There have also been sound arguments made that the first few poems seem to have been set in a certain order by the poet to offer a preview of the themes that he will pursue throughout the course of his poems.

Meter

One of Catullus' lasting legacies to Roman poetry is the variety of meters he used to write his verses. Since this book is designed to get students of all ages ready to **read** Catullus, we will not here study the meters in depth. To be sure they are beautiful and knowledge of them helps you appreciate the poems. But they are best experienced by reading out loud, and comprehension should come first. In the next section we have outlined the meters you will meet in this book. If you read the poems aloud and take longer to say long syllables (we have put in long marks for you) and pass over short vowels more quickly, you should get most of the effect. Your teacher will help you with the specifics.

SOME TRANSLATIONS OF CATULLUS

Catullus is frequently translated and imitated. It is often useful to read a few different translations and then compare them to the Latin. Where do you agree with the translator? Where not? It is always a wonderful way to show the inadequacy of any translation and the pure satisfaction of being able to read a poem in its original. Here are a few translations you might consider for this exercise, though any translation can be of merit in this regard.

Balmer, Josephine. *Poems of Love And Hate. Catullus.* Tarset, Northumberland: Bloodaxe, 2004.

Copley, Frank O. *Catullus. The Complete Poetry.* Ann Arbor: University of Michigan Press, 1957.

Lee, Guy. *The Poems of Catullus.* Oxford: Oxford University Press, 1990.

Martin, Charles. *The Poems of Catullus.* Baltimore: Johns Hopkins University Press, 1989.

Michie, James. *The Poems of Catullus.* Bristol: Bristol Classical Press, 1989.

Mulroy, David. *The Complete Poetry of Catullus.* Madison: University of Wisconsin Press, 2002.

Swanson, Roy Arthur. *Odi et amo. The Complete Poetry of Catullus.* New York: Macmillan, 1959.

SOME WORKS FOR FURTHER REFERENCE

Ancona, Ronnie. *Writing Passion: A Catullus Reader.* Wauconda, Ill.: Bolchazy-Carducci Publishers, 2004.

Arnold, Bruce, et al. *Love and Betrayal. A Catullus Reader.* Upper Saddle River, N.J.: Prentice Hall, 2000.

Bender, Henry, and Phyllis Young Forsyth. *Catullus: Expanded Edition.* Wauconda, Ill.: Bolchazy-Carducci Publishers, 2005.

Ferguson, John. *Catullus.* Oxford, New York: Oxford University Press, 1988.

Fitzgerald, William. *Catullan Provocations. Lyric Poetry and the Drama of Position.* Berkeley and Los Angeles: University of California Press, 1995.

Fordyce, C. J. *Catullus. A Commentary.* Oxford: Clarendon Press, 1961

Forsyth, Phyllis Young. *The Poems Of Catullus: A Teaching Text.* Lanham, Md.: University Press of America, 1986.

Garrison, Daniel H. *The Student's Catullus.* 2nd edition. Norman: University of Oklahoma Press, 1989; 2nd edition 1995.

Harrington, Karl Pomeroy. *Catullus and His Influence.* Boston, Mass.: Marshall Jones Company, 1923.

Havelock, Eric Alfred. *The Lyric Genius of Catullus.* Oxford: B. Blackwell, 1939.

Jaro, Benita Kane. *The Key.* Wauconda, Ill.: Bolchazy-Carducci Publishers, 2002. [Novel based on the life of Catullus.]

Quinn, Kenneth. *Catullus: An Interpretation.* New York: Barnes & Noble, 1973.

Quinn, Kenneth, ed. *Approaches to Catullus.* New York: Barnes & Noble, 1972

Quinn, Kenneth. *The Catullan Revolution.* Ann Arbor, Mich.: University of Michigan Press, 1971.

Quinn, Kenneth, ed. *Catullus: The Poems.* Revised edition. New York: St. Martin's Press, 1970.

Ross, David O. *Style and Tradition in Catullus.* Cambridge: Harvard University Press, 1969.

Small, Stuart G. P. *Catullus, a Reader's Guide to the Poems.* Lanham, Md.: University Press of America, 1983.

Thomson, D. F. S. *Catullus: A Critical Edition.* Chapel Hill, N.C.: University of North Carolina Press, 1978. [excellent on manuscript tradition.]

Wiseman, T. P. *Catullus and His World: A Reappraisal.* New York: Cambridge University Press, 1985.

CATULLAN METERS

Catullus used, and enjoyed using, a variety of meters with impressive names—hendecasyllabic, choliambic, glyconic, Sapphic, greater Asclepiadean, iambic trimeter (both regular and "catalectic"), galliambic, dactylic hexameter, and elegiac.

In this volume we meet only hendecasyllabic, choliambic, elegiac, dactylic hexameter, and sapphic. To try to treat all these meters would detract from the purpose of a transitional reader, which is to get the student to the point where s/he can facilely **read** the ancient author in question. Yet meter is important as it adds so much to poetry.

We have decided, therefore, to concentrate on two meters—hendecasyllabic and elegiac. These are the most common of Catullus' meters and are fairly easy to master. We give you the basic pattern only for choliambic and sapphic. What follows is an introduction to those meters and the very basics of learning to scan a line of Catullan verse.

ENGLISH METER

In English we determine the meter of a line by the natural stress that each word has. Any English speaker can hear the rhythm of

/ ∪ ∪ / ‖ / ∪ ∪ /
Roses are red, violets are blue

Here the stress in English is indicated by the symbol / and unstressed syllables are indicated by ∪.

Notice how we naturally pronounce "violets" as "vilets" to fit the meter. We do it unconsciously, fitting the language to the meter.

Or take the first line from Poe's "The Raven"

/ ∪ / ∪ / ∪   / ∪ / ∪ / ∪   /   ∪ / ∪
Once upon a midnight dreary, while I pondered, weak and weary

Notice here that once we get the pattern going (long, short, long, short) we naturally fall into it and monosyllabic words like "and" (which can have stress or not, depending on where they are in a sentence) just sort of naturally fall into place.

Notice too that there is a natural break after "dreary." Try reading the line and putting a break after, say, "midnight," to hear what an unnatural break sounds like. Where is there another natural break in this line? Remember this concept. A natural pause like this is called a "caesura."

LATIN METER

Latin meter is just about this natural. The big difference is that it is not based on word stress. It rather sees each syllable of each word as "long" or "short" based on the vowel that is in that syllable and the meter ends up being a fairly predictable series of longs and shorts.

How do you determine if a syllable is "long" or "short"? The basics are easy, but the exceptions are numerous. We will give you the basics only, and this will get you started.

Long Syllables

a) contain a vowel that is naturally long (these are marked in this textbook). Almost all diphthongs (e.g. "ae" or "au") are long by nature.

or

b) contain a vowel that is followed by two consonants (even if one word ends in a single consonant and the next word starts with one). There are exceptions, but these can wait for later.

   Consider this famous line of Catullus, "Let's live, my Lesbia, and let's love."

   Vīvāmus mea Lesbia atque amēmus.

In the above example, the vowels long by nature have a long mark over them and the ones long by position are marked with bold italic fonts to show why they are long by position.

Short Syllables

a) contain a vowel that is naturally short or, more simply, are all those syllables that are not long!

Elision

This is the one "trick" we will mention. Most simply put, elision is the blending together of words. You do it all the time in your everyday speech. Consider this bit of after-school talk:

   "Hey, djya see Marty?"
   "Nope, he's left."
   "Whendja see 'im?"

Elision is very common in poetry and, unlike after-school talk, is used by the poet to elevate the language of the poem. The rules are fairly complex, but elision occurs basically when one word ends in a vowel, diphthong, or *m* and the next word begins with a vowel, diphthong or *h*. Remember! These rules are the basics. Your teacher may choose to show you more. But this will give you the sense of elision.

Consider the line again. We have put a symbol where there is elision.

   Vīvāmus mea Lesbia → atque → amēmus.

After the elisions take place, the line would read as follows:

   Vīvāmus mea Lesbi' atq' amēmus

A poet of Catullus's skill almost assuredly does not do this just "to make the meter fit." Notice how it binds Lesbia and the idea of "let's love" physically together in the line. You say it as if it were one phrase—one idea. It certainly was such for Catullus!

Summary

How should you use all this information? For now, we recommend that you use this basic information on meter just as a guide to the fact that meter exists. You will find that the best thing to do is to memorize a few lines, paying careful attention to long marks and elisions. It will be useful to locate and mark the elisions before you start reading out loud. Take longer saying the long syllables than the short ones and you will be fine for now. Intensive study of meter is at the discretion of the teacher.

CATULLAN METERS

Symbols

_ = a long syllable, containing a vowel long either by nature or by position

U = a short syllable

× = "anceps," marking a syllable that can be either long or short

/ = start of a new foot

‖ = caesura, a break or pause in the meter

A. Hendecasyllabic About two-thirds of the poems between 1 and 60 (the "polymetric poems") are written in this meter. It is also called "Phalaecean."

As the name suggests in Greek, there are eleven syllables to the line. This is invariable. But there are a few substitutions allowed. This is the most common pattern given for memorization. Substitutions occur in the first or last "foot" only.

_ _ / _ UU / _ U / _ U / _ ×
_ U
U _

To return to our line:

_ _ / _ UU / _ U / _ ⁀U / _ U
Vīvāmus mea Lesbi' atq' amēmus

B. Elegiac This is a very popular meter throughout Latin poetry. It consists of a full dactylic hexameter line followed by a truncated hexameter line called a "pentameter." The pattern is then repeated in pairs. Note that two shorts routinely resolve into a single long.

_ ŪŪ / _ ŪŪ / _ ŪŪ / _ ŪŪ / _ UU / _ × (hexameter)

_ ŪŪ / _ ŪŪ / _ / ‖ _ UU / _ UU / × (pentameter)

Take the famous poem in this book where Catullus says he both hates and loves at the same time.

Ōdī et amō. Quārē id faciam, fortasse requīris.

Nesciō, sed fierī sentiō et excrucior.

Here it is with the elisions marked and the elegiac meter noted.

_ U U / _ _ / _ UU / _ _ / _ U U / _ U
Ōd' et amō. Quār' id faciam, fortasse requīris.

_ UU / _ UU / _‖ _ U U / _ UU / ×
Nesciō, sed fierī ‖ senti' et excrucior.

Note: In this poem, the final -o of nescio is short, despite being long by nature. As we said, exceptions are everywhere!

C. **Sapphic** This is a complicated meter, taken from the Greek of the poet Sappho and used by Catullus to describe how he fell in and out of love with Lesbia. It is a four line pattern.

$\_ \cup \_ \underset{\smile}{} / \_ \cup \cup \_ / \cup \_ \_$ (three times)

$\_ \underset{\smile\smile}{} \_ \times$

D. **Choliambic** This meter also comes from the Greek and was associated frequently with satire and diatribe. Here is its pattern:

$\underset{\smile}{} \_ / \cup \_ / \underset{\smile}{} \_ / \cup \_ / \cup \_ / \_ \times$

CATULLUS 1

To Cornelius—A Dedication

Before You Read What Catullus Wrote

Introduction

Many ancient works of poetry begin with a dedication. Sometimes it is to a patron who offered the poet financial or moral support. Here Catullus offers his "little book" (*libellus*) to Cornelius Nepos. Nepos was a historian and biographer but more importantly to Catullus, he was a friend. Friendship was especially important to Catullus and his circle and it was seen as crucial to their literary inspiration. Nepos had apparently seen Catullus' early works and had reacted favorably.

Since this poem concerns dedicating a book of poetry, it is a good idea to know what a Roman book looked like. The picture below shows ancient scrolls, made of papyrus, and various writing implements. You can see how books looked when rolled up and stored, how they were unrolled to read, and various writing implements. To make a roll, papyrus was soaked and cut into strips which were then joined together to make one sheet of varying length. The sheets were then joined together to produce a roll and the sheets were polished with pumice to provide the author with a smooth writing surface. The objects to the right are wax tablets and are the sort of thing Catullus would have used to write first drafts and revisions. They are mentioned in Poem 50, below.

Fig. 2.
Ancient Scrolls and Writing Implements

Meter: Hendecasyllabic

Keep This Grammar in Mind   PARTICIPLES

Before each poem in this book you will encounter a section like this. The grammar we choose to review in each instance is grammar that you will encounter in reading the poem at hand.

1. **Review of Participles**

    Let's begin with a review of participles. For now, let's review what the more common ones look like and how to translate them. Remember that a participle is a verbal adjective, so that it agrees in Gender, Number and Case with a noun.

- **Present Active Participle**

  Catullus, libellum expoliēns . . . "Catullus, polishing the book . . . "

  Note: This is a third declension adjective. Its ablative singular can end in either -e or -ī.

- **Perfect Passive Participle**

  Libellus, ā Catullō expolītus . . . "A book, polished by Catullus . . . "

  Note: This sort of participle is declined like "bonus, -a, -um." The most literal translation, "having been polished" preserves the sense of "Perfect" (having) and "Passive" (been) but can be somewhat awkward.

  Note too that most verbs in Latin have no Perfect Active Participle. The only time you can say "having done something" is with a deponent verb. Thus, "secūtus" translates "having followed," not "having been followed."

- **Future Active Participle**

  Catullus, libellum expolītūrus . . . "Catullus, about to polish the book . . . "

  Note: This also declines like "bonus, -a, -um."

Now It's Your Turn

Exercise A

Using verbs found in this poem (see vocabulary below if you have to), and from the common verb *scrībō, -ere, scrīpsī, scrīptum,* translate these phrases properly. Throughout the book any vocabulary that is not included in the pull-out section will be found accompanying the exercise itself.

1. vir libellum dōnāns . . .

2. virī libellōs dōnantēs . . .

3. libellus ā Catullō dōnātus . . .   **dōnō, -āre, -āvī, -ātum = dō, dare, dedī, datum**

4. Catullus Cornēliō libellum dōnātūrus . . .

5. libellus multōs annōs manēns . . .   **libellus, -ī,** m. little book

6. libellus multōs annōs mānsūrus . . .

7. libellus ā Catullō scrīptus . . .

8. Cornēlius libellum doctum scrībere ausus . . .

9. Catullus, libellum scrīptūrus . . .

10. Catullus, libellum scrībēns . . .

2. **The Genitive Case**

You are certainly familiar with the genitive case and know that it is almost always translated "of." But there are a few special uses that need some attention on your part, since Catullus uses it often in a variety of ways. There are two uses here that will reappear in Catullus.

a. **Genitive of Price**

In this poem Catullus writes:

Rūmōrēsque senum sevēriōrum / omnēs **ūnius** aestimēmus **assis**!
"Let's reckon all the rumors of those rather fierce old men as **worth a single penny**."

Notice the difference between the "regular" use of the genitive in *senum sevēriōrum* ("the rumors **of** those rather fierce old men") and the special translation of a genitive of price.

b. **Genitive with Special Words**

Catullus makes frequent use of a construction combining a neuter singular with a genitive.

In this poem you will read

   neuter   gen.

quidquid hoc **libellī**

literally   "whatever this is of a little book"
more naturally   "this little book, such as it is"

See the exercise below in "Stopping for Some Practice" for more ways Catullus uses the genitive.

HELPING YOU TO READ WHAT CATULLUS WROTE

Questions

Before you start the poem, stop and think about to whom books are dedicated today. What are some fairly regular choices for dedications? If you don't know, check a few books before going on. You may wish to check the dedications at the front of this book as well. It will help you focus on the importance of the choice Catullus makes here.

Vocabulary

1. **lepidus, -a, -um** charming
   libellus, -ī, m. diminutive of *liber, librī,* m. book, see "After Reading What Catullus Wrote," below.

2. **āridus, -a, -um** dry, parched, thirsty
   pūmex, -icis, f. pumice stone
   modo adv. just now, recently
   expoliō, -īre, -īvī, -ītum to polish

4. **aliquid** something
   nūgae, -ārum, f. trifles

5. **Ītalus, -a, -um** Italian
   audeō, -ēre, ausus sum (semi-deponent) to dare
   explicō, -āre to explain

6. **aevum, -ī,** n. age, history, time
   trēs, tria three
   carta, -ae, f. a sheet of papyrus, but here, "volume."

7. **doctus, -a, -um** learned, knowledgable
   labōriōsus, -a, -um full of work

8. **quisquis, quidquid** whatever
   quāliscumque, quālecumque of whatever sort

9. **patrōna, -ae,** f. patroness, protectress
   perennis, -e lasting a long time, eternal
   saeclum, -ī, n. age, generation

Notes

1. **Cui:** the dative of *quis.*
   dōnō = *dō*

2. **pūmice:** pumice stone was used to smooth the ends of the *libellus*
   modo be careful to distinguish this adverb from *modō,* the abl. sing. of *modus, -ī,* m. manner, method. You can only tell the difference by the final long vowel.

3. **namque** = *nam*

4. **putāre meās nūgās esse:** indirect statement, "to think that my trifles were."

5. **cum** Look carefully. Is this controlling an ablative or a clause?
   ūnus = *sōlus*

7. **Iuppiter** "By Jove!" This emphatic calling on the highest god shows the strength of Catullus' feelings. Later you will see examples of the high premium Catullus and his friends put on the display of learning in one's writing.

8. **Quārē** = *ergō,* or *igitur,* "therefore."
   tibi a reflexive pronoun, "have this book for yourself."

9. **maneat:** a subjunctive expressing a wish, sometimes called the "optative subjunctive." Translate as "May it . . ."
   virgō: the muse watching over Catullus' poetry: "maiden."

Making Sense of It

To get you used to poetic word order, please read the poem through first as it is printed below.

Note that words in parentheses such as **(hunc)** are words added by the editors to help you follow the Latin. Latin is very fond of leaving things out, a process called "gapping," and we will supply these words when necessary. When you read the poem in its unchanged form, however, you will note that such words are often omitted by the poet.

In this first version you read we have marked noun/adjective pairs with similar fonts to help you understand what words "go together."

1   Cui dōnō (hunc) lepidum novum libellum

2   *ārida* modo *pūmice* expolītum?

3   Cornēlī, tibi: namque tū solēbās

4   *meās* esse aliquid putāre *nūgās*

5   iam tum, cum (tu), ūnus Ītalōrum, ausus es explicāre

6   omne aevum **tribus cartīs**

7   **doctīs**, Iuppiter, et **labōriōsīs**.

8   Quārē habē tibi quidquid quālecumque (est) hoc libellum.

9   maneat, ō patrōna virgō, plūs **ūnō** perenne **saeclō.**

Stopping for Some Practice   CATULLUS AND THE GENITIVE

Catullus makes frequent use of a construction combining a neuter singular with a genitive.

In Poem 1 you read **quidquid hoc libellī**

literally:	whatever this is of a little book.
more naturally:	this little book, such as it is

Exercise B

Fill in each blank with the genitive of the phrase requested. Give a literal and then a more natural translation of each. Use the wordbank (below) to help you with any unfamiliar words.

Ex. quantum est **hominum beātiōrum** (hominēs beātiōrēs)

      literal: how much there is of rather blessed people
      natural: however many happy people there are

1. quantum est _____ (hominēs venustiōrēs)

2. quidquid est _____ (cacchinī)

3. quantum _____ (pecūnia) habēs

4. tantum _____ (pecūnia) habeō

5. quantum est _____ (bāsia)

6. tantum _____ (bāsia)

7. quidquid _____ (bonum)

8. quidquid _____ (malum)

9. aliquid _____ (ineptiae)

10. nihil _____ (cēna)

Wordbank

bāsium, -ī, n. kiss
cacchinī, -ōrum, m. pl. laughter
ineptiae, -ārum, f. pl. foolishness
pecūnia, -ae, f. money
venustus, -a, -um charming

WHAT CATULLUS ACTUALLY WROTE

You are now ready to read the poem exactly as Catullus wrote it for his audience. You have already seen most of the vocabulary and notes in the previous version. Refer back to them if you need to. One additional note is added below.

Notes

10. **plūs ūnō . . . saeclō** an ablative of comparison, "more than . . ."
   perenne, technically a predicate adjective, modifying *quod*, "may this thing last, everlasting, etc." But in English, you can make better sense by translating it as an adverb, "forever."

As It Was

1. Cui dōnō lepidum novum libellum

2. āridā modo pūmice expolītum?

3. Cornēlī, tibi: namque tū solēbās

4. meās esse aliquid putāre nūgās

5. iam tum, cum ausus es ūnus Ītalōrum

6. omne aevum tribus explicāre cartīs

7. doctīs, Iuppiter, et labōriōsīs.

8. Quārē habē tibi quidquid hoc libellī

9. quālecumque; quod, ō patrōna virgō

10. plūs ūnō maneat perenne saeclō.

AFTER READING WHAT CATULLUS WROTE

Thinking about How the Author Writes   DIMINUTIVES

Many languages have special forms that indicate something is a smaller version of something else. Diminutives often imply affection and "cuteness" as well.

So in Spanish *perro* is "dog" but *perrito* is "puppy," and you might affectionately call your father *papito* instead of *papá*. We have them in English too. A "piglet" could never be confused with a "pig" and if you had an hour you might finish reading a "booklet" but never a "book." Other examples in English include: kitchenette, gosling (a lot smaller than a goose!) and diskette.

Catullus is very fond of diminutives. He often makes them up to be clever. Their meaning is usually fairly clear if you know the word they derive from, however.

- **NB** Latin diminutives tend to have the letter "l" in their endings, e.g., *-lus, -lum, -ella*.

Stopping for Some Practice   DIMINUTIVES

Exercise C

Try filling in the following chart. All the words are used by Catullus in his other poems.

Diminutive	Meaning	Latin Word from Which it is Derived
libellus	"little book"	liber, book
ocellus		oculus, eye
frīgidulus (adjective)		frīgidus, cold
labellum		labrum, lip
flosculus		flōs, flower
misellus (an adjective)		miser, wretched, love sick
amīculus		amīcus, friend
versiculus		versus, a verse, line of poetry

Thinking about What You Read

Catullus is careful to give us some hints as to his sense of humor and playful use of language in this introduction.

1. First make a list of phrases and words that Catullus uses to describe his book.

2. What if these words are describing not only the physical book but also the poems it contains? What is he telling us about his poetry?

3. Why would Catullus use words that might indicate that the poems or their author were unimportant?

CATULLUS 51

LOVE'S POWER

BEFORE YOU READ WHAT CATULLUS WROTE

Introduction

Here Catullus tells of the overwhelming effect Lesbia has on him. Many believe this to be the first of the poems Catullus wrote about Lesbia, and that it describes seeing her for the first time. Catullus gives a detailed description of the physical changes that come over him when he looks on Lesbia. It is a powerful description of the feeling of being in love. At the end of the poem, Catullus chastises himself for having too much leisure.

Before you go on, stop and think about the first time you met that "special someone." What were you feeling? How do films depict that moment when lovers first meet?

Meter: Sapphic

Keep This Grammar in Mind   GENITIVE AND DATIVE PRONOUNS

Review of Genitive and Dative Pronouns—Singular

Pronouns are very frequent in Catullus' poetry. Many of the forms are immediately clear since they have the forms of regular adjectives. Forms such as *quās, quōrum, nostrōrum, ipsās,* or *hōs* will not give you much trouble.

The genitive and dative singular, however, are frequently irregular.

First and Second Person Personal Pronouns

	Gen. Sing	Dat. Sing
I (ego)	meī	mihi (commonly "mī")
you (tū)	tuī	tibi

There is a large group of pronouns, however, where

The Genitive singular ends in   **-ius**.
The Dative singular ends in   **-ī**.

These irregular forms are important to know because they occur so frequently in Latin. Here are some common singular pronouns in the genitive and dative case.

• **NB** these forms are the same for all three genders.

	Gen. Sing.	Dat. Sing.
he, she, it (is, ea, id)	eius	eī
this (hic, haec, hoc)	huius	huic
that (ille, illa, illud)	illīus	illī
who (quī, quae, quod)	cuius	cui
each (quisque, quaeque, quidque)	cuiusque	cuique

Now It's Your Turn

Exercise A

Translate each sentence with the new pronoun in place of bold noun.

1. Ille vir fortis esse **puellae** vidētur.   (That man appears brave **to the girl**.)

    a) Ille vir fortis esse **mihi** vidētur.   <u>That man appears brave to me.</u>

    b) Ille vir fortis esse **tibi** vidētur.   _____

    c) Ille vir fortis esse **huic (feminae)** vidētur.   _____

    d) Ille vir fortis esse **illī (virō)** vidētur.   _____

2. Amīcus **puerī** laetus est.   (**The boy's** friend is happy.)

    a) **Cuius** amicus laetus est?   _____

    b) Amīcus **eius** laetus est.   _____

    c) Amīcus **illīus** laetus est.   _____

    d) Amīcus **huius** laetus est.   _____

Now try it the other way around. Put the pronoun into the correct form to parallel the sample sentence.

3. Ōtium **Catullō** molestum est.   (Leisure is troublesome **for Catullus**).

    a) To whom is leisure troublesome?   <u>cui_____</u>

    b) to this (person)   _____

    c) to him   _____

    d) to you   _____

    e) to me   _____

4. Ancilla cēnam **dominae** parāvit.   (The slave-woman prepared dinner **for her mistress**.)

   a) For whom did she prepare dinner?   _____

   b) for this (man)   _____

   c) for that (woman)   _____

   d) for that (man)   _____

   e) for each (person)   _____

HELPING YOU TO READ WHAT CATULLUS WROTE

Vocabulary

1. **pār, paris** equal

2. **fās** (indeclinable), n. right; divinely allowable
   superō, -āre to surpass

3. **adversus** prep. + acc. opposite

4. **identidem** again and again

5. **sēnsus, -ūs**, m. sense, feeling

6. **ēripiō, -ere, -uī, ēreptum** to snatch away

7. **aspiciō, -ere, aspexī, aspectum** to look upon, look at
   supersum, -esse to be left

8. **vōx, vōcis**, f. voice

9. **torpeō, -ēre** to be numb
   tenuis, -e thin

10. **artus, -ūs**, m. limb, joint
    dēmānō, -āre to flow down
    sonitus, -ūs, m. sound

11. **tintinō, -āre** to ring
    geminus, -a, -um twin

12. **tegō, -ere, texī, tectum** to cover

13. **ōtium, -ī**, n. leisure
    molestus, -a, -um troublesome

14. **exsultō, -āre** (w. abl.) to rejoice in
    nimium adv. too much
    gestiō, -īre, -īvī to be elated, to delight

15. **prius** adv. previously, in the past
    beātus, -a, -um happy, blessed

16. **perdō, -ere, perdidī, perditum** to ruin

Notes

1. Remember, **mī** = *mihi*.
   vidētur It is very important to remember that the verb *videō*, in the passive, means "seem" or "appear," rather than "is seen."

2. **ille** *ille/hic, illa/haec* when used alone to refer to a noun already mentioned can often be translated not "this" or "that," but simply "he" or "she."
   sī fās est Catullus feels very strongly about the good fortune of the man he is describing, but he uses this phrase to avoid offending the gods, who are not fond of being surpassed by mere mortals.

5. **dulciter** an adverb formed from the third declension adjective *dulcis*, sweet, "sweetly."
   quod The antecedent of this relative pronoun is imprecise. It is the whole situation Catullus has described in lines 1–5: "a thing that . . . "

Making Sense of It

1   Ille (vir) mihi pār deō esse vidētur,

2   ille, sī fās est, superāre deōs (vidētur),

3   (is) quī sedēns adversus tē

4   identidem spectat et audit

5   (tē) dulciter rīdentem, quod **omnēs sēnsūs**

6   ā **mē miserō** ēripit: nam simul atque, Lesbia,

7   tē aspexī, mihi superest nihil

8   vōcis in ōre.

9   Sed lingua (mea) torpet, **tenuis flamma**

10   sub **artūs (meōs)** dēmānat, *sonitū suō*

11   tintinant aurēs (meae), **gemīnā nocte**

12   oculī (meī) teguntur.

13   Ōtium, Catulle, tibi molestum est;

14   ōtiō exsultās nimiumque gestīs:

15   ōtium prius et rēgēs et **beātās urbēs**

16   perdidit.

Stopping for Some Practice   USES OF THE DATIVE

You will remember that the dative is generally translated "to" or "for" and its most common use is the indirect object.

Here we will look at other uses of the dative case, the **Dative of Separation**, the **Dative of Possession**, and the **Dative of Reference**.

The Dative of Separation

The Dative of Separation works like the **opposite of an indirect object.**
The word in the dative is not the one **to whom** something is given, but the one **from whom** something is taken. When Lesbia's pet bird dies, Catullus complains to the shades of the underworld:

Tam bellum **mihi** passerem abstulistis.   You have taken away so beautiful a sparrow **from me.**

The Dative of Possession

The **Dative of Possession** usually occurs with a **form of** *esse* as the main verb.

Mihi est liber.	Literally More Naturally	There is a book **to me.** I have a book.
Lesbiae multī amantēs sunt.	Literally More Naturally	**To Lesbia** there are many lovers. Lesbia has many lovers.

The Dative of Reference

The **Dative of Reference** is an umbrella term for a use of the dative not easily classified as something else. It means that the statement is true **with reference to** the noun in the dative.
Sometimes a form can be understood as either a dative of reference or a dative of possession. "To" or "for" or "with reference to" may work for a translation, but imagination is often called for.

Haec **Catullō** maxima laetitia est.	This is the greatest happiness **for Catullus.**
Ōtium **tibi** molestum est.	Leisure is troublesome **to you / in your experience / as far as you are concerned.**

Exercise B

Translate each sentence and identify the use of the dative. Use the wordbank (below) to help you with any unfamiliar words.

1. Haec **illī** maxima laetitia est.

2. Fortūna **mihi** tē abstulit.

3. **Mihi miserō** omnia bona ēripuistī.

4. Quae vīta **tibi** manet?

5. **Cui** labella mordēbis?

6. Quintia formōsa est **multīs hominibus**.

7. Tu **mī (= mihi)** es vīlior et levior quam Quintia.

8. **Lesbiae** et **Catullō** multa bāsia sunt.

9. Pulchritūdō Lesbiae sēnsūs **mihi** ēripit.

10. Ōlim sōlēs candidī **tibi** fulsērunt.

11. Tam fuit malum **mihi**, ut nihil facere possem.

Wordbank

auferō, auferre, abstulī, ablātum to take away
bāsium, -ī, n. kiss
ēripiō, -ere, ēripuī, ēreptum to snatch away
formōsus, -a, -um beautiful
fortūna, -ae, f. fortune, Fate
fulgeō, -ēre, fulsī to shine
labellum, -ī, n. lip
laetitia, -ae, f. happiness
levis, -e light, trivial
mordeō, -ēre, momordī, morsum to nibble, bite
ōlim once
pulchritūdō, -inis, f. beauty
Quintia (a name)
quod because
sēnsus, -ūs, m. sense, feeling
sōl, sōlis, m. sun
vīlis, -e cheap

WHAT CATULLUS ACTUALLY WROTE

• **NB:** You have already seen much of this vocabulary just above. If you need to, refer back to it. The notes below will help you with this version of the poem.

Vocabulary	Notes
2. **dīvus, -a, -um** divine	2. **dīvōs** Catullus uses an adjective in place of a noun, *dīvus* (a divine being) = *deus*.
	3. The **tē** does double duty. It is the object of the preposition *adversus*, and object of the verbs in line 4.
	5. **dulce** = *dulciter*. Using a neuter accusative adjective in place of an adverb is common in Latin poetry. "Laughing a sweet thing" = "laughing sweetly." **rīdentem** modifies *tē* (line 3). **miserō** with *mihi* (line 6), dative of separation. **omnīs** = omnēs. This use of *-īs* for third declension *-ēs* in the accusative plural is fairly common in the poets.
	6. **simul** = simul atque
	7. **est super** = superest
	8. This line is missing in all the manuscripts of Catullus. The reading offered is the generally agreed-upon best guess of what the line might have said. The brackets indicate text supplied by editors.
	10. **suōpte** the ending *-pte* makes the adjective *suus, -a, -um* more intense, "very own eyes."
	11. **tintinant** An example of onomatopoeia. This poetic device is explained at the end of this chapter in "Thinking about How the Author Writes."
12. **lūmen, -inis,** n. light, lamp	11–12. **lūmina** = oculī. This phrase literally says "my eyes are covered with twin night." See below for other poetic devices that appear in this poem.

As It Was

Now try reading it as Catullus wrote it.

1   Ille mī pār esse deō vidētur,

2   ille, sī fās est, superāre dīvōs,

3   quī sedēns adversus identidem tē

4   spectat et audit

5   dulce rīdentem, miserō quod omnīs

6   ēripit sēnsūs mihi: nam simul tē,

7   Lesbia, aspexī, nihil est super mī

8   <vōcis in ōre.>

9   Lingua sed torpet, tenuis sub artūs

10   flamma dēmānat, sonitū suōpte

11   tintinant aurēs, geminā teguntur

12   lūmina nocte.

13   Ōtium, Catulle, tibi molestum est:

14   ōtiō exsultās nimiumque gestīs:

15   ōtium et rēgēs prius et beātās

16   perdidit urbēs.

AFTER READING WHAT CATULLUS WROTE

The poetic word order is intricate in this poem. Consider lines 9–12

    9   Lingua sed torpet, tenuis sub artūs
    10   flamma dēmānat, sonitū suōpte
    11   tintinant aurēs, geminā teguntur
    12   lūmina nocte.

Bracketed Word Order

A. **tenuis** sub artūs **flamma** dēmānat

A delicate flame drips down through my limbs

The first phrase is a classic example of bracketed word order, "sandwiching," where an adjective and a noun enclose a longer phrase—here *sub artūs*. This sort of word order is extremely common in Latin poetry. It was also found in everyday Latin. Consider phrases like **magnā cum laude** or **summā cum celeritāte**. To be able to translate Latin poetry with some ease you have to get used to this common device.

Hint: when you see an adjective and there is no word near it which it can modify, start to think that this might be a "sandwich" and make a good guess that the noun is coming later.

Look at these examples from other places in this book

1.   fulsērunt vērē **candidī** tibi **sōlēs** (8.6)

     "Truly bright suns shone for you then."

2.   tam tē bāsia multa bāsiāre
     vēsānō satis et super **Catullō** est. (7.9–10)

     "To kiss you that much is enough and more than enough for crazy Catullus."

3.   **paucīs,** sī tibi dī favent, **diēbus**

     In a few days, if the gods show you their favor.

4.   **nulla** in tam magnō est corpore **mīca** salis (86.4)

     "There is no grain of salt in so large a body."

     This is a double example with **nūlla . . . mīca** bracketing **magnō . . . corpore**.

Metonymy

B. **gemină** teguntur lūmina **nocte**

My eyes are covered over with a twin night

Here the poetic word order allows Catullus to make a poetic point by juxtaposing two words with almost opposite meanings—*lūmina* and *nocte*, "lights" and "night." But there is more at work here than just clever positioning. Poetic word choice also plays a role since, if Catullus had used the more common *oculus* instead of *lūmen*, "light," then positioning it next to *nocte* would not have been nearly as effective. The use of "light" for "eye" is an example of **metonymy**.

Metonymy is a common device in Catullus' poetry. We will return to it later in the book. For now, remember that it is **a device where the poet calls something by a related name, or by naming one of its attributes.**

Metonymy is a fairly broad term, and can cover such expressions as

- "The White House announced today . . . " (White House = President)
- "The pen is mightier than the sword."
- "Remember the Alamo!"

Can you see how metonymy works in the other two examples?

So in these two small lines we have discovered **bracketed word order, poetic juxtaposition of words,** and **metonymy.** The true test of the poetic value of such a line as this is the very fact that it sounds so bad in literally translated English—"and twin are covered lights by night." It is only by reading it in the original Latin that you can experience all the poet's craft.

Onomatopoeia

C. TinTinanT aurēs, **geminā** TegunTur
   lūmina **nocTe.**

My ears ring, my eyes are covered with a twin night

Onomatopoeia is a Greek term for a word that, when said aloud, reproduces the sound implied by its meaning. Thus "tintinant" sounds, when spoken, like the tinkling or ringing of a bell. This effect is heightened by the frequent repetition of the "t" sound in these two lines.

Here are a few English words that are onomatopoetic. Can you list 7 others?

1. Screech
2. Ululation (= howling)
3. Ding dong
4.
5.
6.
7.
8.
9.
10.

Transferred Epithet

The phrase "**geminā** teguntur lūmina **nocte**" is translated as "my lights (= eyes) are covered with twin night."

We have dealt above with the metonymy, but you should notice here also that "twin" is, in fact, misplaced—technically, Catullus has two eyes, not "twin darknesses." But poetry is poetry and this sort of enhanced diction, where the adjective modifies a different word than we would expect, is referred to a using a "transferred epithet."

You may, in fact, have had your English teacher mark this wrong in your compositions, calling it a "misplaced modifier." Just another advantage poets have over writers of prose!

Thinking about What You Read

1. Why do you think Catullus begins this poem by talking about a third party, instead of himself or Lesbia?

2. Notice that Catullus leaves out all the words for "my" in the third stanza, depersonalizing his description of the symptoms of love. Why do you think he does this?

3. In lines 9–12 Catullus describes only the <u>physical</u> symptoms of being with his beloved but he implies the <u>emotional</u> effects. List the symptoms and tell what emotion might be causing each.

4. Many readers of this poem have tried to guess what Catullus wrote in line 8, which is missing from the manuscripts. It is now your turn to become a literary detective.

   a) Write a translation of lines 6–8, supplying your own idea of what the missing line might have said, different from the normal conjecture, printed above.

   b) The more adventurous might try to supply the missing line in Latin. We know from the meter of the poem that it was five syllables long.

5. Catullus had great admiration for the work of the Greek poet Sappho. His made-up nickname for his lover is "Lesbia," a tribute to the island of Lesbos where Sappho wrote her poetry. Elsewhere Catullus even calls a woman who shares his own literary taste "more learned than the Sapphic muse." And any of his friends who read this poem knew immediately that it was a translation of a poem by Sappho. Can a translation of someone else's poem be an effective vehicle for the expression of personal emotion?

6. Lines 1–12 are a direct translation of the poem by Sappho. Catullus adds the final stanza to her words. Why do you think he did so? Many of us think leisure is a fine thing, so why is leisure bad for him right now? What has it done to Catullus as lover/poet?

CATULLUS 5

To Lesbia—Let's Seize the Day

Before You Read What Catullus Wrote

Introduction

Catullus was a love poet who lived in Rome. Like some other Roman love poets he was in love with a married woman who treated him poorly and as a result he calls himself *miser*, or "wretched," in many of his poems. Here, though, he is ecstatic. Things are going well for him and for Lesbia, his lover, but some people are clucking their tongues at the pair. Lesbia, after all, was married and had quite a reputation around Rome as a loose woman.

In this poem Catullus tells his love (and the reader as well) that none of that matters. *Vīvāmus mea Lesbia, atque amēmus!*

"We should live and love while we can," he says, "since soon our sun will set and we will be dead."

There is no end to the number of kisses that a lover should get from his mistress and Catullus reels off some numbers to prove it. But he warns that he and Lesbia should scramble the exact number (as if they were stacked coins or markers on an abacus) so that those who wish them ill will not have any accurate data to use to cast spells against them (*invidēre*, line 13).

Meter: Hendecasyllabic

Keep This Grammar in Mind   Gerundive to Show Necessity

In this poem, when trying to say that all must die, Catullus says

nōbīs . . . nox **est** perpetua ūna **dormienda**

"There is one perpetual night that we must sleep."

Latin uses the **gerundive plus the verb esse** to indicate necessity or obligation. This is sometimes called the "**Passive Periphrastic**." The agent—the person who has to do the thing—is expressed by the **dative**.

Example:

Liber mihi legendus est. The book must be read by me. = I must read the book.

Now It's Your Turn

Exercise A

Matching. Select the correct gerundive from the list below to complete the passive periphrastic. Pay attention to the genders!

1. Cui libellus meus _____ est? (To whom should my book be given?)

2. Mihi multae rēs _____ sunt. (I have to do many things.)

3. Carthāgō _____ est. (Carthage must be destroyed.)

4. Medicō hominēs aegrī _____ sunt. (A doctor must care for sick people.)

5. Tibi equus _____ est. (You must find the horse.)

6. Marcō casa nova _____ est. (Marcus must paint the new house.)

7. Urnae puellīs _____ sunt. (The girls must fill the jars.)

A. complendae
B. cūrandī
C. dēlenda
D. dōnandus
E. faciendae
F. inveniendus
G. pingenda

Exercise B

Translate the following phrases based on lines in Catullus' own poems. Use the wordbank (next page) to help you with any unfamiliar words.

1. Ūna nox perpetua nōbīs dormienda est.

2. Hoc tibi faciendum est.

3. Cēna Catullō paranda erit.

4. Catullō obdūrandum est.

5. Puellīs puerīsque laus Diānae canenda est.

6. Librī malī in igne ustulandī sunt.

Wordbank

canō, -ere to sing
cōgitātiō, cōgitātiōnis, f. thought
ignis, ignis, m. fire
laus, laudis, f. praise
obdūrō, -āre to be tough
perpetuus, -a, -um everlasting
ustulō, -āre to burn

Exercise C

Here are some English words and names in common usage. First give the meaning of the word as it is used today. Then give the literal translation of the word as if it were a Latin periphrastic expression.

English Word	English Definition	Latin Translation
agenda	a list of things to be acted upon or voted upon	"things that must be done"
reverend		
dividend		
amanda		
miranda		
addendum		
legend		
referendum		

HELPING YOU TO READ WHAT CATULLUS WROTE

Vocabulary

1. **vīvō, -ere** to live

2. **rūmor, -ōris,** m. rumor, popular opinion
   senex, senis, m. old man
   sevērus, -a, -um severe, stern, harsh

3. **aestimō, -āre** to reckon
   as, assis, m. "a penny"

4. **occidō, -ere, occidī** to set, sink
   redeō, -īre to return

5. **semel** adv. once
   brevis, -e short, brief
   lūx, lūcis, f. light

6. **perpetuus, -a, -um** everlasting

7. **bāsium, -ī,** n. kiss
   deinde then

8. **dein = deinde**
   centum a hundred

9. **alter, -era, -erum** another, a second

11. **conturbō, -āre** to mix up, jumble

12. **invideō, -ēre** to envy (perhaps with the idea of casting the evil eye on something)

Notes

1. **vīvāmus**: the first of three hortatory subjunctives in the first three lines, all translated "Let's."

2. **sevēriōrum**: comparative adjective, *rather severe*

3. **omnēs**: modifies **rūmōrēs** (line 2), but it is placed next to **ūnius** to highlight the contrast.
   Ūnius assis: See, "Keep in This Grammar in Mind" for Poem 1 to be reminded of this "Genitive of Price." An *as* was the smallest Roman coin.

5. **brevis lūx**: Catullus uses this phrase to refer to our life, comparing its brevity to a single day. It is a very rich phrase since, after death, the sun comes back, but the dead remain "set."

6. For help translating this gerundive phrase, see "Keep in This Grammar in Mind," above.

9. **usque** can be an adverb or a preposition and has many meanings. Here, the sense of the whole phrase is probably "still another thousand" or "all the way to another thousand."

10. **cum . . . fēcerīmus**: future perfect indicative, "when we have made." The future perfect is commonly used before a future to refer to the first of two future events.

11. **nē sciāmus**: negative purpose clause, see "Thinking about How the Author Writes," below.

12. **nē quis . . . possit**: another negative purpose clause. Why is *aliquis* shortened to *quis*? After certain negative words, this is a regular occurrence. "After *sī, nisi, num,* and *nē,* all the *ali*'s fall away."

13. **cum tantum sciat esse**: indirect statement, *when he knows that there are this many.*

Making Sense of It

1 Vīvāmus, mea Lesbia, atque amēmus.

2 Rūmōrēsque *senum sevēriōrum*

3 omnēs **ūnius** aestimēmus **assis**!

4 Sōlēs occidere et redīre possunt.

5 Nōbīs, cum semel occidit **brevis lūx**,

6 **nox** est **perpetua ūna dormienda**.

7 Dā mī bāsia mille, deinde centum,

8 dein mille altera, dein secunda centum,

9 deinde usque altera mille, deinde centum.

10 Dein, cum mīlia multa fēcerīmus,

11 conturbābimus illa (bāsia), nē sciāmus,

12 aut nē *quis (=aliquis) malus* invidēre possit,

13 cum tantum sciat esse basiōrum.

As It Was

Here are the actual words of the poem, unchanged. Notice that there are only two small changes from the previous version. You are already reading the poems just as their original audience did!

1   Vīvāmus, mea Lesbia, atque amēmus.

2   Rūmōrēsque senum sevēriōrum

3   omnēs ūnius aestimēmus assis!

4   Sōlēs occidere et redīre possunt.

5   Nōbīs, cum semel occidit brevis lūx,

6   nox est perpetua ūna dormienda.

7   Dā mī bāsia mille, deinde centum,

8   dein mille altera, dein secunda centum,

9   deinde usque altera mille, deinde centum.

10   Dein, cum mīlia multa fēcerīmus,

11   conturbābimus illa, nē sciāmus,

12   aut nē quis malus invidēre possit,

13   cum tantum sciat esse basiōrum.

AFTER READING WHAT CATULLUS WROTE

Thinking about How the Author Writes	NEGATIVE PURPOSE AND RESULT CLAUSES

This poem contains both result and purpose clauses. Both kinds of clauses use **ut** if they are not negative, but if they are negative (e.g. "I did this so that you wouldn't find out." or "You are so kind that I couldn't ever repay you.") they no longer act the same.

1. **Negative purpose clauses are introduced by** *nē* **= so that not, lest.**

   Consider the example from this poem:

   Conturbābimus illa (bāsia) **nē sciāmus**, aut **nē** quis (= aliquis) malus invidēre **possit.**

   We will jumble those kisses together lest we know (how many there are) or lest any bad-minded person be able to give us the evil eye.

2. **Negative result clauses are introduced by** *ut* **and a negative word. As always, look for a "so" word, e.g. tam, tantum, sīc, or the like, in the main clause.**

   Tam bene illa bāsia conturbāvimus, **ut nēmō** nōbīs invidēre **posset.**

   We jumbled those kisses so well that no one was able to give us the evil eye.

Stopping for Some Practice	PURPOSE AND RESULT CLAUSES

Exercise D

Your turn—translate the following and tell whether the clause is purpose or result. Use the wordbank (below) to help you with any unfamiliar words.

1. Multam aquam ferimus nē quis sitiat.

2. Tantam aquam tulimus ut nēmō sitīrētur.

3. Catullus puellae fabulam narrat nē ineptus videātur.

4. Catullus tam pauper est ut nūllam cēnam amīcīs dare possit.

5. Nōlī audax esse, nē Nemesis poenās ā tē reposcat.

6. Catullus Lesbiam suam tam ferventer amābat ut dormīre nōn posset.

7. Catullus vult tē tam multa bāsia dare ut nēmō curiōsus ea numerāre possit.

Wordbank

audāx, audācis (one-termination adj.) bold, presumptuous

bāsium, -ī, n. kiss

cūriōsus, -a, -um inquisitive, curious

fabula, -ae, f. story

ferventer furiously, intensely

ineptus, -a, -um foolish

narrō, -āre to tell

Nemesis (goddess, punisher of arrogance)

numerō, -āre to count, number

pauper, pauperis (one-termination adj.) poor

poena, -ae, f. punishment

reposcō, -ere to demand

sitiō, -īre to thirst

vidēre (in passive) to seem

CATULLUS 7

To Lesbia—How many Kisses? Once More

Before You Read What Catullus Wrote

Introduction

This is a terrific poem, but you need to know several things before you start to read it. Catullus belonged to a circle of friends, mostly poets, whom Cicero called the "Neoterics" or "the New Crowd." These poets put a lot of value on being able to refer to obscure places or figures, confident that members of the group were sophisticated enough to "get it." Members of the "out crowd" of course would be too dense to catch on to this style of writing, known as Alexandrianism.

So, in this poem, when Catullus wants to say that the kisses should be as numerous as the grains of sand on a beach, not just any beach will do. He specifies that it lies in North Africa, in Libya (**Libyssae harēnae**) at "silphium-producing Cyrene." Be sure to refer to the map in the front of the book for the place names.

Silphium was a special plant used in cooking and medicine that was very abundant at Cyrene. It was so overharvested by the Romans that it went extinct. Not surprisingly, Nero is on record as having insisted on eating the last remaining plant. The plant was so important that the people of Cyrene put it on their coins. The coin below is from Cyrene and features the plant on its reverse. On the front is an image of Zeus Ammon. Note the horns above his ears, a sign of this particular god. More on this in a moment.

Fig. 3.

Front of Cyrene Coin   Reverse of Cyrene Coin

Then Catullus goes on to say how big the beach is. But he has to do this in a "Neoteric" way. It stretches "between the oracle of sweltering Jupiter" and the "sacred tomb of old Battus." If you were one of Catullus' friends you knew that the oracle was the oracle of Ammon, consulted by Alexander the Great, who then minted coins depicting himself as Zeus Ammon, complete with Ammon's ram horns (see illustration, below). You knew that the oracle was very hard to get to because of its desert location and that the tomb of Battus was the sacred resting spot of the first king of Cyrene and lay more than 300 miles from Ammon. A lot of sand indeed! And, of course, a lot of kisses.

Never forget that Lesbia was supposed to "get" the allusions and elevated references as well. She is loved as much for her intellect as for her other obvious charms.

Meter: Hendecasyllabic

Fig. 4.
Alexander Coin

HELPING YOU TO READ WHAT CATULLUS WROTE

Vocabulary

1. **quaerō, -ere, quaesīvī, quaesītum** to ask

2. **quot** how many
   satis enough

3. **numerus, -ī**, m. number
   Libyssus, -a, -um Libyan
   harēna, -ae, f. sand

4. **iaceō, -ēre** to lie
   Cyrēnae, -ārum, f. pl. Cyrene

6. **ōrāclum, -ī**, n. oracle. (sometimes written as *ōrāculum*)
   aestuōsus, -a, -um blazing hot, sweltering

7. **sacer, -cra, -crum** sacred, holy
   sepulcrum, -ī, n. grave, tomb
   vetus, -eris (one-termination adj.) old

8. **sīdus, -eris**, n. star

10. **furtīvus, -a, -um** furtive, stealthy

11. **bāsium, -ī**, n. a kiss
    bāsiō, -āre to kiss

12. **super** adv. above, more

13. **cūriōsus, -a, -um** curious
    pernumerō, -āre to count

14. **fascinō, -āre** to put a spell on someone/thing

Notes

2. **bāsiātiōnēs** An odd-sounding substitute for *bāsia*: "kissifications."
   superque "and more than enough." Remember that *-que*, attached to the end of a word, is the same as putting the word *et* in front of that word. Compare line 12.

3. **quam magnus numerus**: "as large as the number (of the Libyan sand) that"

4. **lāsarpīciferīs**: "silphium-producing." For details see "Before You Read." Always read these sections before you start the poem.

6. **Iovis . . . aestuōsī**: "sweltering Jove" is a poetic way to refer to Ammon, an Egyptian god. Is Jove actually sweltering? This sort of Neoteric wordplay is called a "transferred epithet."

7. **Battī veteris**: see introduction for an explanation of the geography Catullus is describing here.

8. **quam sīdera multa**: "as many as the stars that"

12. **vēsānō** = *īnsānō*

Making Sense of It

The word order may be a bit tricky in this poem. Try reading it in this configuration first. We have rearranged the words so that related words are next to each other. The text is arranged in sense units and by degree of importance. The main parts of a sentence are generally farthest left—e.g., in the last stanza *Sīc* and *possunt* go together and govern the rest of the clauses. Subordinate clauses are farther to the right and if they are in pairs, they appear in a small column.

Look for the words in bold. They show you the structure of the phrases and of the poem as a whole.

Basically, the poem is structured as follows: "You ask how many (**quot**) kisses are enough? As many (**Quam**) as lie on the shore in North Africa or as many (**quam**) as there are stars on a still night. That is how many (**tam**) are enough!"

1   Quaeris, Lesbia,

2   **quot** bāsiātiōnēs tuae sint satis superque mihi.

3   **Quam** magnus numerus Libyssae harēnae

4   iacet lāsarpīciferīs Cyrēnīs

5   inter

6   ōrāclum Iovis aestuōsī

7   et sacrum sepulcrum Battī veteris;

8   aut **quam** multa sīdera,

9   cum tacet nox,

10   furtīvōs amōrēs hominum vident:

11   **tam** multa bāsia tē bāsiāre

12   vēsānō Catullō satis et super est.

13   Sīc   nec cūriōsī pernumerāre

14   nec mala lingua fascināre

15   possunt

WHAT CATULLUS ACTUALLY WROTE

Notes

12. **possint**: potential subjunctive, *could*. It has two subjects: *cūriōsī* and *mala lingua*. So many kisses are mixed up that no one could possibly count them and nobody's evil tongue could possibly cast a spell.

As It Was

1   Quaeris, quot mihi bāsiātiōnēs

2   tuae, Lesbia, sint satis superque.

3   Quam magnus numerus Libyssae harēnae

4   lāsarpīciferīs iacet Cyrēnīs

5   ōrāclum Iovis inter aestuōsī

6   et Battī veteris sacrum sepulcrum;

7   aut quam sīdera multa, cum tacet nox,

8   furtīvōs hominum vident amōrēs:

9   tam tē bāsia multa bāsiāre

10   vēsānō satis et super Catullō est,

11   quae nec pernumerāre cūriōsī

12   possint nec mala fascināre lingua.

CATULLUS 87

A Love beyond Compare

Before You Read What Catullus Wrote

Introduction

This is a little poem, only two couplets long, in which Catullus praises his faithfulness to Lesbia. The first couplet is in the third person, and the second couplet is addressed directly to Lesbia in the second person. He does not say so directly, but by mentioning only his own faithfulness, Catullus seems to suggest that Lesbia's behavior toward him is not as true.

Meter: Elegiac

Keep This Grammar in Mind   Indirect Statement and the Accusative Pronoun *sē*

The Latin pronoun *sē* is very commonly used as the accusative subject of an infinitive verb in indirect statement. Its translation depends on the subject of the main verb:

Fēmina negat **sē** librum habēre.	The woman denies **that she** has the book.
Puer dīxit **sē** ventūrum esse.	The boy said **that he** would come.
Parentēs eius putant **sē** omnia scīre.	His parents think **that they** know everything.

Some infinitives are formed by using a participle and *esse*.

- Puer dīxit sē opus **factūrum esse**. The boy said that he would do the work.
- Puer dīxit opus **factum esse**. The boy said that the work had been done.

When an infinitive uses *esse*, a Latin author will often leave it out, so that the previous sentences may also appear as follows with no change in meaning:

- Puer dīxit sē opus **factūrum**.
- Puer dīxit opus **factum**.

Now It's Your Turn

Exercise A

Translate the following sentences. Use the wordbank (below) to help you with any unfamiliar words.

1. Catullus dīcit sē Lesbiam amāre.

2. Lesbia dīcēbat sē Catullum amāre.

3. Lesbia narrat sē esse miseram.

4. Catullus dīxit sē lectīcam comparāvisse.

5. Poēta scrīpsit sē bāsia velle.

6. Ille vir putat sē mīrificē loquī.

7. Cornēlius putat Catullī carmina esse bona.

8. Catullus spērat amīcōs suōs Lesbiae aliquid nūntiātūrōs esse.

9. Lesbia et amīcus nesciēbant sē spectārī.

10. Catullus nēgat ūllam puellam tam amātam. (also, what is missing?)

11. Puella mea dīcit sē mihi nūbere velle.

Wordbank

aliquid something
bāsium, -ī, n. kiss
carmen, -minis, n. song, poem
comparō, -āre to acquire, get together
lectīca, -ae, f. a litter. Slaves routinely carried their masters through the streets of Rome in these long, covered devices that we would today describe as stretchers covered with an awning to protect the rider from the elements.
loquor, loquī to speak
mīrificē adv. wonderfully
narrō, -āre to tell
negō, -āre to deny
nesciō, -īre to not know
nūbō, -ere to be married
nūntiō, -āre to announce
spērō, -āre to hope
ūllus, -a, -um any

Vocabulary

1. **mulier, mulieris,** f. woman
   vērē adv. truly

3. **fidēs, -eī,** f. faith
   ūllus, -a, -um any
   foedus, foederis, n. bond
   umquam adv. ever

4. **reperiō, -īre, repperī, repertum** to find

Notes

1. **sē** Remember what we just discussed above concerning the translation of this word. What word in this sentence determines how *sē* is translated?
   tantum ... quantum These correlatives are literally translated "so much ... how much." A more natural way is "as much ... as."

3. **tanta ... quanta** as great ... as.

4. **tuō** your = "of you."

Making Sense of It

1   *Nūlla mulier* vērē dīcere potest sē tantum amātam (esse),

2   quantum ā mē Lesbia amāta est.

3   **Nūlla fidēs** in ūllō foedere umquam fuit **tanta,**

4   **quanta** in amōre tuō ex parte meā **reperta** est.

Stopping for Some Practice   TRANSLATING INDIRECT STATEMENT

Remember that in indirect statement an infinitive can be translated two different ways depending on the tense of the main verb.

Fēmina **negat** sē librum **habēre.**   The woman **denies** that she **has** the book.

Fēmina **negāvit** sē librum **habēre.**   The woman **denied** that she **had** the book.

*   Notice that the same infinitive is translated differently because the tense of the main verb has changed.

Exercise B

Here are the sentences from Exercise A rewritten with the verb in a different tense. Retranslate each sentence using the main verb in the new tense given here. If you need vocabulary, it is listed in the wordbank for Exercise A.

Example: Version A   Catullus dīcit sē Lesbiam amāre.   Catullus says that he loves Lesbia.
             Version B   Catullus dīxit sē Lesbiam amāre.   Catullus said that he loved Lesbia.

1. Lesbia dīcit sē Catullum amāre.

2. Lesbia narrāvit sē esse miseram.

3. Catullus dīcit sē lectīcam comparāvisse.

4. Poēta scrībit sē bāsia velle.

5. Ille vir putāvit sē mīrificē loquī.

6. Catullus spērābat amīcōs suōs puellae Lesbiae aliquid nuntiātūrōs esse.

7. Lesbia et amīcus nesciunt sē spectārī.

WHAT CATULLUS ACTUALLY WROTE

As It Was

1   Nūlla potest mulier tantum sē dīcere amātam

2   vērē, quantum ā mē Lesbia amāta mea est.

3   Nūlla fidēs ūllō fuit umquam foedere tanta,

4   quanta in amōre tuō ex parte reperta meā est.

AFTER READING WHAT CATULLUS WROTE

Thinking about How the Author Writes

SIMPLE WORDS

One of the features of Catullus' style is the way he uses simple vocabulary in a complex way. An example is found in the last line of this poem. The phrase *amōre tuō* is more complex than it appears. Remember that Latin, like English, uses possessive adjectives in place of first and second person genitive pronouns. For example, we say, "my book—*liber meus*," not "the book of me—*liber meī*."

In the phrase *amōre tuō* the adjective *tuō* is replacing a genitive, but it is unclear at first glance whether it is a <u>subjective</u> genitive (your love = the love that you have) or an <u>objective</u> genitive (the love of you = the love that another has for you). Only with the phrase *ex parte meā* does it become apparent that the more hopeful interpretation that Lesbia faithfully loves Catullus must be abandoned. *Amōre tuō ex parte meā* taken together must mean "the love of you from my side."

Let's practice some more with these tricky pronouns and possessive adjectives:

Exercise C

In each of the following sentences, choose the correct pronoun or adjective form to translate the underlined word.

1. I saw <u>my</u> friend.   (mē, meum, meus)
2. She gave <u>me</u> a book.   (mē, mihi, meum)
3. Where is <u>your</u> book?   (tū, tuus, tuum)
4. They have <u>their own</u> books.   (sē, suōs, sibi)
5. You always praised <u>my</u> trifles.   (mē, meās, mihi)
6. I don't care that old men know <u>we</u> are kissing.   (nōs, noster, nostrōs)
7. <u>Your</u> kisses are never enough for crazy Catullus.   (tū, tua, tē)
8. <u>You</u> will be sad when no one loves you.   (tū, tē, tua)

9. Lesbia says a lot of mean things <u>to me</u>.   (mē, mī, meum)

10. She will never be forgetful <u>of me</u>.   (mē, meī, meum)

11. <u>My</u> friend Varus invited <u>me</u> to meet <u>his</u> girlfriend.   (The choices for 11 and 12 are below the underlined word)

mē	mē	sē
meus	meus	suam
meum	meum	suī

12. <u>My</u> girlfriend says that <u>she</u> wants to marry me.

mē	sē
mea	suam
meam	sibi

Thinking about What You Read

1. This poem is about unrequited love. What is your understanding of that term and what are some possible ways it can make a person feel? Go back and look at this poem to see if you can find any language that suggests Catullus' emotions.

2. Another way to view this same poem hinges on the word *foedus*, which can mean a contract or a binding legal document. Catullus frequently speaks of love in these terms. To what extent is a love affair a contract? What is expected from each party?

    After you have thought about this, go back to the poem and look for "legal" language and tone. How is the tone of this poem different from the tone of the other love poems you have read so far?

CATULLUS 8

To Himself—Getting over Lesbia

Before You Read What Catullus Wrote

Introduction

In this poem Catullus admits (probably not for the first time and probably not for the last time) that his love affair with Lesbia is over. A reader of Catullus has to believe that he has told himself this many times over, only to be filled with joy at a later date when Lesbia smiled at him or told him they would meet.

Notice that the first part of the poem (lines 1–12) is addressed to himself and he then turns and directly addresses Lesbia (*Valē, puella!*). If you read the poem as if it were a little play that we are allowed to watch, you will really become wrapped up in the emotions Catullus is showing.

Perhaps you have broken up with someone you thought you loved, or perhaps one of your friends has had this experience. Think about the emotions you went through. We all expect pain and depression but were there others? Perhaps you have noticed anger, resolve, or a desire for revenge? Are things sometimes said at such times that the speaker later wishes s/he could retract? Why is that?

Before you go on to read this poem, give some serious thought to these very human emotions. What else do spurned lovers feel?

Meter: Choliambic

Keep This Grammar in Mind   Giving Commands in Latin

Catullus expresses commands in several ways and you see several of them in this poem alone. Let's review the whole spectrum of giving commands in Latin.

Imperative

Dā! Give! **Lūgēte!** Mourn!

Present Subjunctive

Dēsinās! (You should) stop!

Negative commands can use

1) The imperative of **nōlō**

   Nōlī amīcum meum revocāre.   Be unwilling to call my friend back.
   Don't call my friend back.

2) *Cavē* + subjunctive

   Cavē sīs.   Beware of being. = Don't be.

3) **Nē (nec/neque) + imperative**

   Nec sedē, nec iacē.   Neither sit, nor lie.

4) **Nē + perfect subjunctive**

   Note that while the perfect subjunctive is used, you still translate it as a present imperative.

   Nē id fēceris!   Don't do that!

   Nē Lesbiam oppugnāveris!   Don't attack Lesbia!

Now It's Your Turn

Exercise A

Translate the following, identifying the form of the imperative verb or equivalent. These are all based on Catullus' actual words. Use the wordbank (below) to help you with any unfamiliar words.

1. Miser Catulle, dēsinās ineptīre.

2. Nuntiāte, comitēs, meae puellae pauca nōn bona dicta.

3. Sī mihi nōn crēdis, crēde frātrī tuō.

4. Cavē despuās meās precēs.

5. Nec mē fuge, neque sperne.

6. Aut linteum remitte, aut īram meam exspectā.

Wordbank

comēs, comitis, m. companion
dēsinō, -ere to cease, stop
despuō, -ere to spurn
dictum, -ī, n. *verbum*
exspectō, -āre to wait for, expect
ineptiō, -īre to be a fool
īra, -ae, f. anger
linteum, -ī, n. napkin
nūntiō, -āre to announce
paucī, -ae, -a few
prex, precis, f. prayer
remittō, -ere to send back
sector, sectārī to follow after, pursue
spernō, -ere to spurn

NOTES

HELPING YOU TO READ WHAT CATULLUS WROTE

Vocabulary

1. **dēsinō, -ere** to cease, stop
   ineptiō, -īre to be foolish or silly, to play the fool

2. **pereō, -īre** to perish, die

3. **perdō, -ere, -didī, -ditum** to ruin, wreck

4. **quondam** at one time, once
   candidus, -a, -um white, bright
   fulgeō, -ēre, fulsī to shine, glow brightly

5. **ventitō, -āre** to come often or over and over again

6. **quantum** adv. as much as

7. **ibi** there, then
   iocōsus, -a, -um full of fun, playful
   fīō, fierī, factus sum to happen, occur

9. **vērē** adv. truly

10. **inpotēns, -entis** (one-termination adj.) powerless, weak

11. **sector, -ārī, -ātus sum** to follow

12. **obstinātus, -a, -um** stubborn, determined
    perferō, -ferre, -tulī, -lātum to carry on to the end, to endure
    obdūrō, -āre to be tough, to brace yourself for something, to be tough

13. **valeō, -ēre, valuī** to thrive, fare well

14. **requīrō, -ere, requīsīvī, requīsītum** to ask for, seek

15. **invītus, -a, -um** unwilling

Notes

1–2. **dēsinās, dūcās**: the equivalent of imperatives. See "Before You Read What Catullus Wrote." **dūcās** here means "consider."

2. **quod vidēs perīsse**: indirect statement, "what you see has perished."

4. **fulsēre = fulsērunt.** How can you tell that this is not an infinitive? See "Thinking about How the Author Writes," immediately below.

5. **ventitābās**: In Latin the verbal ending **-itō** implies frequent repetition. **Ventitō** is derived from *veniō*.

7. **cum** Look carefully. Is this controlling an ablative or a clause?
   ibi An excellent example of the sort of (intentional?) vagueness that can exist in poetry. Does Catullus mean "there," in the place to where Lesbia led Catullus or is it "then, when many jokes used to occur?" Or might he intentionally mean both at once?

10. **nōlī** This word is often paired with an infinitive to mean "Don't . . . Here it is best translated literally, "be unwilling."

11. **sectāre**: imperative. Deponent verbs have imperatives that look like infinitives, so be careful!

15. **nec rogābit invītam = nec rogābit tē, sī tū es invīta**

Making Sense of It

First try reading the poem in this format. Then move directly to the unchanged poem that follows.

1 Miser Catulle, dēsinās ineptīre,

2 et dūcās id quod vidēs periisse

3   perditum esse.

4 Quondam sōlēs candidī tibi fulsēre,

5 cum ventitābās quō puella dūcēbat,

6   puella amāta ā nōbīs quantum nūlla amābitur.

7 Ibi cum illa multa iocōsa fiēbant,

8   quae tū volēbās nec puella nōlēbat,

9 vērē sōlēs candidī tibī fulsēre.

10 Nunc iam puella nōn vult: tū quoque inpotēns nōlī,

11 nec sectāre (eam) quae fugit, nec miser vīve,

12 sed obstinātā mente perfer, obdūrā.

13 Valē, puella. Iam Catullus obdūrat,

14   nec tē requīret

15   nec rogābit invītam.

HELPING YOU TO READ WHAT CATULLUS WROTE

Vocabulary

16. doleō, -ēre, -uī to mourn, grieve for

17. scelestus, -a, -um wretched, wicked
   vae + dat. or (as here) acc. "Woe on . . . !"

18. adeō, -īre, -iī to go toward, approach

20. bāsiō, -āre to kiss
   labellum, -ī, n. lip
   mordeō, -ēre, momordī, morsum to bite

21. dēstīnātus, -a, -um determined, stubborn,
   resolute

Notes

18. Remember that *videō,* when passive in form,
   is most commonly translated as "seem" or
   "appear."

19. dīcēris: future passive, "will you be said"

20. cui: dative of reference = "whose"

Making Sense of It (CONTINUED)

16 At tū dolēbis, cum nōn rogāberis.

17 Scelesta, vae tē! Quae vīta tibi manet?

18 Quis nunc tē adībit? Cui vidēberis bella?

19 Quem nunc amābis? Cuius esse dicēris?

20 Quem bāsiābis? Cui labella mordēbis?

21 At tū, Catulle, dēstīnātus obdūrā.

WHAT CATULLUS ACTUALLY WROTE

Notes

2. perīsse a shortened, or "syncopated," form for *periisse*
14. nūlla modifying "Lesbia" (the "tu" of the poem), with the simple sense of "not."

As It Was

Now try reading it as Catullus wrote it. If you have to, go back for vocabulary.

1   Miser Catulle, dēsinās ineptīre,

2   et quod vidēs perīsse perditum dūcās.

3   Fulsēre quondam candidī tibī sōlēs,

4   cum ventitābās quō puella dūcēbat

5   amāta nōbīs quantum amābitur nūlla.

6   Ibi illa multa cum iocōsa fīēbant,

7   quae tū volēbās nec puella nōlēbat,

8   fulsēre vērē candidī tibī sōlēs.

9   Nunc iam illa nōn vult: tū quoque inpotēns nōlī,

10   nec quae fugit sectāre, nec miser vīve,

11   sed obstinātā mente perfer, obdūrā.

12   Valē puella, iam Catullus obdūrat,

13   nec tē requīret nec rogābit invītam.

14   At tū dolēbis, cum rogāberis nūlla.

15   Scelesta, vae tē, quae tibī manet vīta?

16   Quis nunc tē adībit? Cui vidēberis bella?

17   Quem nunc amābis? Cuius esse dīcēris?

18   Quem bāsiābis? Cui labella mordēbis?

19   At tū, Catulle, dēstīnātus obdūrā.

AFTER READING WHAT CATULLUS WROTE

Thinking about How the Author Writes

"-ēre" for "-ērunt"

Latin poetry often used the suffix **-ēre** to serve as an alternative for **-ērunt** in the perfect tense.

CAVĒTE!!! Students must be careful to distinguish this from the infinitive ending for the third and especially the second conjugation. In the third conjugation the **-ēre** ending is distinct from the **-ere** ending of the infinitive.

The key in the second conjugation is to notice the stem: **-ēre** on the **second** principal part is the infinitive, on the **third** principal part it is the perfect indicative.

Example:	**ascendere** is "to climb" **ascendēre = ascendērunt** and is translated "they climbed" **monēre** is "to warn" **monuēre = monuērunt** and is translated "they warned."

Exercise B

Pay attention to the form of the underlined word and translate the following. Use the wordbank (following page) to help you with any unfamiliar words.

1. Tēcum <u>sedēre</u> volō fābulāsque tuās audīre.

2. Errantēs in silvā puerī subitō in lupum <u>incidēre</u>.

3. Haec prius <u>fuēre</u>, sed nunc omnia sunt mūtāta.

4. Dīxī mē lectīcam <u>habēre</u>; sed tamen nūllam habeō.

5. Puellae puerīque manūs suās <u>iunxēre</u>.

6. Tū es fīdissima omnium mulierum quae sunt, quaeque <u>fuēre</u>, quaeque erunt.

7. Multae puellae illum flōrem pulchrum <u>optāvēre</u>.

8. Difficile est longum subitō <u>dēpōnere</u> amōrem.

Wordbank

dēpōnō, -ere, -posuī, -positum to put down, let go of
difficilis, -e difficult
errō, -āre to wander
fīdissimus, -a, -um most faithful
flōs, flōris, m. flower
incidō, -cidere, -cidī to happen upon
iungō, -ere, iunxī, iunctum to join together
lectīca, -ae, f. sedan chair, litter chair
lupus, -ī, m. wolf
manus, -ūs, f. hand
mulier, -is, f. woman, wife
mūtō, -āre, -āvī, -ātum to change
optō, -āre, -āvī to choose, select
prius adv. formerly, before
silva, -ae, f. forest
subitō adv. suddenly

Thinking about What You Read   HOW HE MADE THE POEM

It is easy to overlook the structure of a Catullan poem since the poems read as if they are spontaneous outpourings of the heart. But in fact the poems are very carefully put together. This little exercise is designed to help you notice structure in this and future poems.

We have reprinted the poem below for you. Ask your teacher whether you should do this exercise in the book or with a photocopy. Or you might do this on a transparency in class as a group.

Read through the poem once more, and as you go along, circle or highlight repetitions. This works best if you use a different color or marking for each set of repetitions.

What words does Catullus repeat to hold his poem together? Hint: Concentrate on question words and note that the same word in a different case counts as a repetition. Thus, *hominēs, homō,* and *hominibus* would all be marked.

You should also count as repetition, "echo words," which sound a great deal alike but are not exactly alike. See how many of these you can find as well.

1   Miser Catulle, dēsinās ineptīre,

2   et quod vidēs perīsse perditum dūcās.

3   Fulsēre quondam candidī tibī sōlēs,

4   cum ventitābās quō puella dūcēbat

5   amāta nōbīs quantum amābitur nūlla.

6   Ibi illa multa cum iocōsa fīēbant,

7   quae tū volēbās nec puella nōlēbat,

8   fulsēre vērē candidī tibī sōlēs.

9   Nunc iam illa nōn vult: tū quoque inpotēns nōlī,

10   nec quae fugit sectāre, nec miser vīve,

11   sed obstinātā mente perfer, obdūrā.

12   Valē puella, iam Catullus obdūrat,

13   nec tē requīret nec rogābit invītam.

14   At tū dolēbis, cum rogāberis nūlla.

15   Scelesta, vae tē, quae tibī manet vīta?

16   Quis nunc tē adībit? Cui vidēberis bella?

17   Quem nunc amābis? Cuius esse dīcēris?

18   Quem bāsiābis? Cui labella mordēbis?

19   At tū, Catulle, dēstīnātus obdūrā.

CATULLUS 70

PROMISES, PROMISES

BEFORE YOU READ WHAT CATULLUS WROTE

Introduction

Lesbia says she wants to marry Catullus, but he is skeptical. He is not very sure that what she says is trustworthy. Have you ever had the feeling that someone is telling you one thing but really believes another? What are your emotions at a time like this?

Meter: Elegiac

Keep This Grammar in Mind   FUTURE CONDITIONS

This poem contains a type of condition and serves well to begin our review of these important constructions.

Future More Vivid Conditions

Conditions using the **future perfect in the "if clause"** and the **future in the "then clause"** state conditions about the future that are factual and very straightforward.

- If you drop something, it will fall. (Gravity is a law, a fact.)

Future Less Vivid Conditions

Conditions using the **present subjunctive in both clauses** are sometimes called "should/would conditions" because of the way they are translated into English.

They are also called "future less vivid conditions" because they refer to the future without being straightforward. We will use the term Future Less Vivid Condition.

- If you should drop that, it would break. (There is no guarantee that you are going to drop it.)

How to Translate Them

Future More Vivid	present / future If <u>you build</u> it, <u>they will come</u>.
Future Less Vivid	should (were to)/ would If <u>you should build</u> it, they <u>would</u> come. If <u>you were to build</u> it, they <u>would</u> come.

Now It's Your Turn

Exercise A

First identify the condition as a Future More Vivid (FMV) or a Future Less Vivid (FLV) Condition. Then indicate what the tense and mood of the underlined verbs would be in Latin.

>   fut. perf. indic.   fut. indic.
> **Example:**   If you <u>meet</u> Lesbia, you <u>will fall</u> in love. **(FMV Condition)**

1. If you <u>return</u> that gift you stole from me, I <u>will forgive</u> you.

2. If you <u>should return</u> that gift you stole from me, I <u>would forgive</u> you.

3. If something bad <u>happens</u> to you, mother <u>will blame</u> me.

4. If you <u>were to inquire</u> why I do this, I <u>would be silent</u>.

5. If that woman <u>were to be compared</u> to Lesbia, I <u>would laugh</u>.

6. If you <u>bring</u> your own dinner, you <u>will dine</u> well.

7. If he <u>were to smell</u> this perfume, he <u>would desire</u> to buy it.

Exercise B

Now take the verbs that are underlined in Exercise A and translate them into Latin. We have given you the verbs that you need. Be sure you are using the right tense and mood based on the kind of condition it is.

1. (reddō, -ere, reddidī) (ignoscō, -ere)

2. same as #1

3. (accidō, -ere, accidī) (culpō, -āre)

4. (requīrō, -ere) (taceō, -ēre)

5. (comparō, -āre) (rīdeō, -ēre)

6. (afferō, afferre, attulī) (cēnō, -āre)

7. (olfaciō, -ere) (cupiō, -ere)

NOTES

HELPING YOU TO READ WHAT CATULLUS WROTE

Things to Consider before You Read

Sometimes when two people are parting, one of them will say something like, "We should get together for lunch sometime," even though both people know this is not going to happen.

1. What reasons do people have for saying such things?

2. What are some other examples of things people say that they do not really mean?

3. Can you think of examples of things people have told you that you knew were not true? How did you know?

Vocabulary

1. mulier, mulieris, f. woman
nūbō, -ere to be married
mālō, mālle to prefer

3. petō, -ere to seek, ask for

5. cupidus, -a, -um eager, longing

6. ventus, -ī, m. wind
rapidus, -a, -um swift

Notes

2. nūllī = *nēminī*, the dative of *nēmō*, "to no one."
quam "than," connecting *nūllī* and *mihi*.

3. Iuppiter A good example of lover's hyperbole. Jupiter is obviously not going to ask Lesbia to marry him.

4. quod A relative pronoun with no expressed antecedent. We do the same in English: instead of saying "that which," we say "what."

5. amantī It is common in Latin to use a participle, "a loving (one)," in place of a noun, "a lover."

6. oportet "it is fitting" or "(he) ought"

Making Sense of It

1   Mulier mea dīcit sē nūbere mālle

2   nūllī quam mihi,

3   Nōn sī Iuppiter ipse sē petat.

4   (Sīc) dīcit, sed quod mulier dīcit

5   cupidō amantī,

6   in ventō et rapidā aquā scrībere oportet.

Now read the poem in its original form. The word order is a little trickier but you can refer to the rearranged version just above for help. Try to think why Catullus arranged the words the way he did. What effects are created by putting certain words next to each other or bracketing other phrases?

WHAT CATULLUS ACTUALLY WROTE

As It Was

1   Nūllī sē dīcit mulier mea nūbere mālle

2   quam mihi, nōn sī sē Iuppiter ipse petat.

3   Dīcit; sed mulier cupidō quod dīcit amantī,

4   in ventō et rapidā scrībere oportet aquā.

AFTER READING WHAT CATULLUS WROTE

Thinking about How the Author Writes   WORD PLACEMENT AND IMAGES

1. What words are emphasized by being put out of their normal word order? It would help a great deal to read the poem aloud, or to have your teacher read it to you, so you can hear how words are emphasized by the meter.

2. Notice that Latin poets can enrich a line by putting adjectives beside nouns that they do not modify. Give an example of this from line 3.

3. What does Catullus mean by the final image?

Thinking about What You Read

1. When do people say things that they don't really mean?

2. Why would Catullus believe or not believe Lesbia's claim?

3. What is the importance of the phrase *cupidō amantī* in understanding the relationship between Catullus and Lesbia?

CATULLUS 72

CATULLUS SENSES A CHANGE IN LESBIA

BEFORE YOU READ WHAT CATULLUS WROTE

Introduction

Catullus senses a change in Lesbia. You have probably sensed changes in friends, family members, or loved ones. How did you feel? Are feelings like these always good indicators of what is going on in a relationship?

Meter: Elegiac

Keep This Grammar in Mind   COMPARATIVES AND SUPERLATIVES

Adjectives and adverbs both come in "degrees." Catullus uses them a great deal so you should be sure you know how to recognize them and translate them.

Positive	Comparative	Superlative
ADJECTIVES		
sweet dulcis, -e	sweeter dulcior, -ius	sweetest dulcissimus, -a, -um
happy beātus, -a, -um	happier beātior, -ius	happiest beātissimus, -a, -um
ADVERBS		
sweetly dulciter	more sweetly dulcius	most sweetly dulcissimē
happily beātē	more happily beātius	most happily beātissimē

In Latin you generally form them by adding the following to the adjective's stem or base:

	Comparative	Superlative
Adjective	-ior, -ius	-issimus, -a, -um
Adverb	-ius	-issimē

Things to Remember

- A form like "impēnsius", in this poem, can be a neuter adjective OR an adverb, both comparatives.

- Comparative adjectives decline like 3rd declension nouns with the -ior M/F and the -ius for the Neuter. The stem is -ior. Thus —

	M/F	N	M/F	N
Nom.	vīlior	vīlius	vīliōrēs	vīliōra
Gen.	vīliōris	vīliōris	vīliōrum	vīliōrum
Dat.	vīliōrī	vīliōrī	vīliōribus	vīliōribus
Acc.	vīliōrem	vīlius	vīliōrēs	vīliōra
Abl.	vīliōre	vīliōre	vīliōribus	vīliōribus

- Adverbs never add endings.

Now It's Your Turn

Exercise A

Using the word in parentheses, choose the right answer.

1. Lesbia is prettier (pulcher) than other women.

    a. pulchra   b. pulcherrima   c. pulchrior   d. pulchrē

2. Send me a poem (carmen, -inis, n.), sadder (maestus, -a, -um) than any poem of Simonides.

    a. maestum   b. maestius   c . maestior   d. maestissimum

3. Oh! what is a happier (beatus, -a, -um) thing than this?

    a. beātum   b. beātissimum   c. beātiōrum   d. beātius

4. And from me you will receive something even sweeter (suāvis, -e).

    a. suāve   b. suāvis   c. suāvissimum   d. suāvius

Be careful as you meet similar forms in Catullus' poems.

NOTES

HELPING YOU TO READ WHAT CATULLUS WROTE

Vocabulary

1. **quondam** once, formerly
nōscō, nōscere, nōvī, nōtum to know

2. **prae** prep. + abl. before, instead of
Iuppiter, Iovis, m. Jupiter

3. **dīligō, -ere, dīlēxī, dīlēctum** to esteem, love

4. **gnātus, -ī,** m. (= nātus, -ī, m.) literally, "one born," child, son.
gener, -ī, m. son-in-law

5. **cognōscō, -scere, -nōvī, -nitum** to come to know
quārē "for which reason", "and as a result."
etsī adv. even if, although
impēnsē adv. at great cost, immoderately
ūrō, ūrere, ūssī, ūstum to burn

6. **vīlis, -e** cheap
levis, -e light, of no account

7. **quōmodo** adv. how
potis, -e possible
inquam, inquis, inquit etc. to say
inūria, -ae, f. injury, harm

8. **cōgō, -ere, coēgī, coactum** to force
aliquis, aliquid somebody, something
volō, velle, voluī to wish, to want to
minus adv. less

Notes

1. **dīcēbās** the imperfect is important here. What force does it have?
nōvisse the perfect tense of verbs like *nōscō* are translated as present tenses. So here, treat this perfect active infinitive (in an indirect statement) like a present infinitive.

3. **nōn tantum ut . . . sed ut** "not only as . . . but as"
vulgus The common folk. Catullus' love is far beyond that.

4. **gnātōs . . . generōs** The love of a father is pure and not fickle like what Lesbia will find with the *vulgus*. There is a hint here of Roman values, since in all likelihood *gnātōs* means male children, valued more highly than daughters and daughters-in-law are not mentioned.

5. **cognōvī** See note to line 1. "I've gotten to know you now" = "Now I know you."
impēnsius comparative adverb. See "Keep This Grammar in Mind," above.
ūror: deponent or passive? It makes a difference.

6. **multō** "by much"
levior, vīlior both comparatives. See "Keep This Grammar in Mind," above.

7. **potis:** although it is m/f in gender, translate as neuter, "how is **it** possible . . . "
inquis: this verb is "defective." That means it lacks some parts or that certain forms of it are never found.

8. **bene velle:** lit. "to wish someone well." Compare the English "benevolent."

Making Sense of It

First try reading the poem in this format. To help you we have broken it into thought groups.

1   Dīcēbās quondam tē sōlum Catullum nōvisse,

2   Lesbia, (et dīcēbās tē) nōlle tenēre Iovem prae mē.

3   Dīlēxī tum tē nōn tantum ut vulgus (dīligit) amīcam,

4   sed ut pater gnātōs et generōs dīligit.

5   Nunc tē cognōvī: quārē etsī impēnsius ūror,

6   multō mihi tamen es vīlior et levior.

7   Quōmodo potis est, inquis? Quod amantem iniūria tālis

8   cōgit (aliquem) amāre magis, sed (cōgit eum) bene velle minus.

WHAT CATULLUS ACTUALLY WROTE

Notes

1. **nōsse** Shortened (syncopated) form for **nōvisse**
7. **quī** a fairly frequent adverb that means "in what way?" "how?"

As It Was

1   Dīcēbās quondam sōlum tē nōsse Catullum,

2   Lesbia, nec prae mē velle tenēre Iovem.

3   Dīlēxī tum tē nōn tantum ut vulgus amīcam,

4   sed pater ut gnātōs dīligit et generōs.

5   Nunc tē cognōvī: quārē etsī impēnsius ūror,

6   multō mī tamen es vīlior et levior.

7   Quī potis est, inquis? Quod amantem iniūria tālis

8   cōgit amāre magis, sed bene velle minus.

AFTER READING WHAT CATULLUS WROTE

Thinking about How the Author Writes	POETIC USE OF TENSES

Tenses: Catullus does not use his tenses randomly. Verbs are in a certain tense for a reason. First, list the tense of the following verbs from the poem you just read.

dīcēbās
dīlēxī
dīligit
cognōvī
cōgit

Let's look at the force of each tense.

For example, does *dīcēbās* give us a hint about whether Lesbia is still saying the same thing now? He offers you a hint in *quondam*.

And when Catullus uses *dīlēxī* is there a hint about how he feels now? He offers you another hint with *tum*.

This is subtle, but lets you begin to understand what is going on in the poet's head.

CATULLUS 11

END OF THE AFFAIR

BEFORE YOU READ WHAT CATULLUS WROTE

Introduction

Catullus lived in a world where three things were terribly important to him—Lesbia, poetry, and his friends. In this remarkable poem you encounter all three at once, for Catullus asks his friends, Furius and Aurelius, to deliver his final message to Lesbia. And the message is far from loving. Of course, he delivers it in the medium of a poem, so all three themes come together nicely. We have all seen relationships break up and know that they frequently get bitter. The personal, biting rancor that ends the affair of Catullus and Lesbia is testimony to how passionate their feelings had been in the past.

Meter: Sapphic. Note that Catullus uses the same meter to write about the end of the affair that he used above in Poem 51 to write about its beginning.

Keep This Grammar in Mind   INDEPENDENT USES OF THE SUBJUNCTIVE

Always be on the lookout for subjunctives used alone, without a conjunction such as "ut" or "cum." They are very common and grammarians divide them in various ways and assign them many names.

We focus here on the two most commonly used names and provide examples and translations for some other independent subjunctives. What they all have in common is that, unlike the indicative, they are not stating a fact. Instead, they show things like potential, possibility, a wish, or even a suggestion or command.

A. Hortatory and Jussive Subjunctive

Name of Construction	Subjunctive Used	How to translate
Hortatory Subjunctive	Present, 1st plural	"Let's"
Jussive Subjunctive	Present, 3rd singular and plural	"Let her/him" or "Let them"

Examples:

1. Abeāmus.   "Let's go away."

2. Exeat.   "Let him go."

3. Fiat lūx!   "Let there be light." (literally, "Let light be made.")

4. Gaudeāmus igitur!   "Let's rejoice, then!" (Title of a medieval drinking song!)

B. **Other Independent Subjunctives**

- Grammarians use many terms for independent subjunctives such as "volitive," "optative," "potential," and "deliberative."

- As a practical matter, these can be translated easily by using words such as "should," "would," "could," "may," "might," and the like. Consider the following examples:

1.	Dīcat aliquis	"Someone might say"
2.	Id faciam?	"Should I do it?"
3.	Quid scrībam?	"What should I write?"
4.	Aliquis id faciat.	"Someone could do that."
5.	Velīsne cēnāre?	"Would you like to have dinner?"

Now It's Your Turn

A. **What sort of subjunctive is represented in these short sentences?**

   1. Hortatory   2. Jussive

   1. Let's live, my Lesbia, and let's love!

   2. Let the old men think what they want!

   3. Let her live with her boyfriends!

B. **Now identify these Latin examples and then translate them.**

   1. Eāmus Rōmam!

   2. Lesbia amet aliōs virōs!

   3. Legāmus carmina Catullī!

Summary

The poem you are about to read begins with Catullus flattering his two friends, Furius and Aurelius. We are not sure who they were, but they appear in other poems. He states that he knows well that these friends will go to the ends of the earth if he asks them to do so and begins the poem with a catalogue of the places they would surely go for him. We have chosen not to have you translate the itinerary and provide the first three stanzas of the poem in English. You will want to glance at the map in the front of this book to see the places listed—they have little in common except how dangerous and arduous it would be to get there.

So, after building up a picture of how loyal and brave his friends are, Catullus asks them now to do something **really** dangerous—to bring his message of farewell to Lesbia. Here are the first 14 lines of the poem, translated into English:

1   Furius and Aurelius, Catullus' comrades,

2   Whether he will go to the further parts of India,

3   Where the shore is beaten by the echoing eastern wave,

4   Or whether he will go to the Hyrcanians and the soft Arabs

5   Or the Sagae or the arrow-carrying Parthians,

6   Or whether he goes to the waters that the seven-mouthed Nile stains
       with its mud,

7   Or whether he will hike his way across the lofty Alps,

8   Viewing the monuments of great Caesar,

9   The French Rhine, the terrible water of the English Channel,

10   And the Britons living at the end of the world.

11   Prepared to try all these things,

12   Whatever the will of the gods will bring . . .

WHAT CATULLUS ACTUALLY WROTE

Vocabulary

15. **paucī, -ae, -a** few
    nūntiō, -āre to announce

17. **vīvō, -ere** to live
    valeō, -ēre to fare well, to flourish
    moechus, -ī, m. low-life, more specifically, an
       adulterer

18. **complector, -plectī, -plexus sum** to embrace
    trecentī, -ae, -a three hundred

19. **identidem** adv. over and over again, repeatedly

20. **īlia, īlium,** n. pl. flanks, loins
    rumpō, -ere to burst, break

21. **respectō, -āre** to look back on
    ante adv. before, previously

22. **culpa, -ae,** f. fault
    cadō, -ere, cecidī, cāsum to fall
    velut adv. just as, like
    prātum, -ī, n. meadow

23. **ultimus, -a, -um** furthest, here, "at the edge of"
    praetereō, -īre to pass by
    postquam conj. after

24. **tangō, -ere, tetigī, tactum** to touch
    arātrum, -ī, n. plow

Notes

16. **nōn bona dicta** Notice the position, at the end
    of a stanza. Furius and Aurelius are reading
    the poem along in order, thinking they will
    be given a small chore and then, suddenly
    realize they have to relate some "not very nice
    words." The next two stanzas prove that the
    words are not nice indeed!

18. **simul complexa** In his anger, Catullus claims
    Lesbia embraces hundreds at a time. He is
    clearly sick of her infidelities.

20. **īlia rumpēns** Here too Catullus uses
    exaggeration (hyperbole) to say that Lesbia
    is such a voracious lover that she wears
    down even hundreds of men. Remember that
    Catullus' poems were written to be seen by all
    their mutual circle of friends.

21. **meum** modifies *amōrem*
    respectet: What kind of subjunctive? See "Keep
    This Grammar in Mind," above.

22–24. What follows may be easier in the following
    version: "(meum amōrem) quī, Lesbiae culpā,
    velut flōs ultimī prātī cecidit, postquam
    praetereunte arātrō tactus est." The image of a
    tender flower, casually cut down by a passing
    plow is a beautiful metaphor for how Catullus
    views his crushed love.
    quī refers back to the *amor.*
    illius = Lesbiae

As It Was

Having praised his companions, Catullus now addresses his companions directly, telling them what he wants them to do for him.

Note: You are ready to solo! As of this point the book no longer offers "Making Sense of It" sections. You should now be fairly familiar with Catullus' poetic diction and word order. Where problems arise, we have offered help in the notes. Be sure to use them!

15 pauca nūntiāte meae puellae

16   nōn bona dicta.

17 Cum suīs vīvat valeatque moechīs,

18 quōs simul complexa tenet trecentōs,

19 nūllum amāns vērē, sed identidem omnium

20   īlia rumpēns;

21 nec meum respectet, ut ante, amōrem,

22 quī illius culpā cecidit velut prātī

23 ultimī flōs, praetereunte postquam

24   tactus arātrō est.

AFTER READING WHAT CATULLUS WROTE

Thinking about What You Read   CATULLAN POETIC STRUCTURE

It is clear that there is a wide range of emotions here—sadness, rage, nostalgia, and more. But Catullus also carefully sets up Furius and Aurelius by structuring the poem in a certain way. At the beginning of the poem they may think Catullus is asking them one thing. But by the end they know that it is quite something else.

Try to gain some insight into Catullus' craft by answering what follows.

1. Structure of the poem. How does Catullus win Furius and Aurelius over at the start of the poem?

2. Why does he list all the places they would go for him only to have this followed by his real request—"*pauca nūntiāte*"? How "small" is the request in reality? Why does he wait to put "*nōn bona*" until after he has written "*pauca*"?

3. In line 17, *suīs* and *moechīs* are widely separated. When you first see *suīs* what words might you expect ("Let her live with her __?__") and what is the effect once you get to *moechīs*?

4. Why is *trecentōs* at the **end** of line 18?

5. Where else in these lines do you see unexpected word choice or word order for similar effect?

6. Now look at lines 15–24 as a whole. How does Catullus build up images and words so that the tender image of the flower at the end is as effective as possible?

Catullan Vocabulary Practice

Choose the Latin word Catullus would have used to translate the underlined English word.

1. <u>Polished</u> with pumice . . .   (conturbātum, doctum, expolītum, fascinātum)

2. A <u>charming</u> book . . .   (īnsulsus, lepidus, miser, molestus)

3. Stop <u>being a fool</u>.   (bāsiāre, fierī, ineptīre, obdurāre)

4. You have too much <u>leisure</u>.   (mūnus, ōtium, scortillum, ventum)

5. Suns are able <u>to set</u>.   (fascināre, fulsēre, nūbere, occidere)

6. It was <u>touched</u> by a passing plow.   (oblītus, parātus, repertus, tactus)

7. <u>Perhaps</u> you ask . . .   (deinde, fortasse, umquam, vērē)

8. Enough for <u>crazy</u> Catullus . . .   (beātō, lepidō, miserō, vēsānō)

9. The oracle of <u>sweltering</u> Jupiter . . . (acris, aestuōsī, labōriōsī, tenuis)

10. Libyan <u>sand</u> . . .   (avia, bāsia, gemina, harēna)

CATULLUS 86

BEAUTY CONTEST

BEFORE YOU READ WHAT CATULLUS WROTE

Introduction

You will remember that three things were uppermost in Catullus' mind—his poetry, Lesbia, and his friends. We know from other poems that the friends in Catullus' circle, often called the Neoteric Poets, or "newer poets," often presented their girlfriends of the moment to each other and generally wrote poems about their love interest.

In this poem, one of the friends has introduced a certain Quintia. She is, Catullus grants, good looking, but she lacks a certain something that Lesbia surely has.

Meter: Elegiac

Keep This Grammar in Mind

Reviewing a few bits of grammar will help you read this poem more easily.

A. Dative of Reference Once More

You know the dative case is generally translated "to" or "for" and that will take you through most situations. We treated several special translations above in Poem 51.

But the **Dative of Reference** deserves some further study. It tells you something or someone in relationship to which something else is true. In this poem you are told that Quintia is *formōsa multīs*. That is, to many people, she is lovely. And Catullus says: *Mihi candida, longa, rēcta est.* In his opinion, that is, she is fair, tall, and has good posture.

Look at a few other uses:

1.   Haec **illī fatuō** maxima laetitia est. "This is the greatest bliss for that fool."

2.   Malest, Cornificī, **tuō Catullō**. "It is going badly, Cornificius, for your Catullus."

3.   Ō **mihi** nūntiī beātī! "Oh what happy news this is for me!"

B. Irregular Comparatives

For Poem 72 we reviewed comparatives and superlatives. We did not, however, review the irregular forms of these. First there are the ones that do not form according to the normal rules but which keep their basic stem ("lim and rim" rule), and then we have completely irregular forms which change their form entirely.

Lim and Rim Adjectives

Lim: The adjectives such as *facilis* and *difficilis* **should** have superlatives that look like "facilissimus" and "difficilissimus." But in fact they are different. Note that the comparatives are not different at all.

	Comparative	**Superlative**
Adjective	facilior, facilius difficilior, difficilius	facillimus, -a, -um difficillimus, -a, -um
Adverb	-ius	-illimē

In all, six adjectives act this way: *facilis, difficilis, similis, dissimilis, gracilis,* and *humilis.*

Rim: Adjectives that end in "er" in the nominative masculine singular (e.g. *pulcher, -chra, -chrum* or *acer, acris, acre*) have superlatives that end in -errimus, -a, -um.

	Comparative	**Superlative**
Adjective	pulchrior, pulchrius	pulcherrimus, -a, -um
Adverb	-ius	-errimē

Irregular Comparatives/Superlatives That Change Stem

Positive	**Comparative**	**Superlative**
bonus, -a, -um	melior, melius	optimus, -a, -um
malus, -a, -um	peior, peius	pessimus, -a, -um
magnus, -a, -um	māior, māius	maximus, -a, -um
parvus, -a, -um	minor, minus	minimus, -a, -um
multus, -a, -um	plūrēs, plūra (plural most common)	plūrimus, -a, -um

NOTES

WHAT CATULLUS ACTUALLY WROTE

Vocabulary

1. **fōrmōsus, -a, -um** attractive, lovely, shapely
   candidus, -a, -um gleaming white, fair-complexioned
   longus, -a, -um here, as common for the Romans, "tall."

2. **rēctus, -a, -um** "straight"; here, with good posture,
   singulus, -a, -um one by one
   cōnfiteor, cōnfitērī, cōnfessus sum to confess, admit

3. **negō, -āre** to deny
   venustās, -tātis, f. charm, grace. What deity's name lies beneath this attribute?

4. **mīca, -ae,** f. morsel, bit, grain
   sāl, sālis, m. salt

6. **surripiō, -ripere, -ripuī, -reptum** to steal (something) away (from someone)

Notes

3. **tōtum** A neuter adjective can be used as an adverb. Translate "totally."

4. **tam magnō . . . corpore** Just above the lady was tall, and had good posture. By putting in the one word, "magno" here, we now see that Catullus was trying to be polite. Quintia is just too big for his idea of beauty!
   mīca sālis We might say she had no spice in her. What does Catullus mean? What does Lesbia have that Quintia lacks?

5. **pulcerrima** alternate spelling for pulcherrima

5–6. **cum . . . tum** "not only . . . but also"

6. An awkward line. " . . . she has also stolen all the charms (that exist) from everybody."
   omnibus The dative is frequently used with verbs involving taking something away. See the explanation at Poem 51.
   omnīs = omnēs as often in poetry

As It Was

Before you read you might want to jot down a few things that make someone attractive. What today is generally accepted as being "good looking" and what not? What is essential for someone to get "second looks" or to be bragged about? Call this list "Good Looks."

Then write down a list of what someone looks for once one gets beyond mere looks. Call this list "Beyond Good Looks." What character traits make for a truly significant companion? What enhances good looks? And what remains after, as inevitably happens, those looks go away?

We will come back to these lists below. For now, read the poem that follows to get Catullus' view on the subject.

1 Quīntia fōrmōsa est multīs. Mihi candida, longa,

2   rēcta est: haec ego sīc singula cōnfiteor.

3 Tōtum illud "fōrmōsa" negō: nam nūlla venustās,

4   nūlla in tam magnō est corpore mīca sālis.

5 Lesbia fōrmōsa est, quae cum pulcerrima tōta est,

6   tum omnibus ūna omnīs surripuit Venerēs.

AFTER READING WHAT CATULLUS WROTE

Thinking about How the Author Writes   POETIC WORD ORDER

Students sometimes think that poetic word order is so uninhibited that there are no rules at all—that the poet is simply putting words down wherever he feels like doing so. Worse, we are often told that most of the word order is simply "metrī causā," "for the sake of the meter."

If either of these is true, you are probably reading an inferior poet and Catullus was surely not one of these. He takes great pains to arrange his words craftily to help him get his points across. And the present poem illustrates this very well. Once you realize that poetic word order helps, and does not harm, a poem, you will be able to read poems more quickly and with greater pleasure.

Let's look at some examples from this poem.

• Quīntia fōrmōsa est **multīs. Mihi** candida, longa,

    The words in bold are deliberately put together to enforce the contrast. A lot of people might think one thing, Catullus says, but here is my opinion. And he even does it with **alliteration**, the repetition of consonant sounds—here, an "m."

- **Lesbia fōrmōsa est**, quae cum pulcerrima tōta est,

Notice how the first three words of this line are the same as the beginning of the poem, with only the subject changed.

- tum **omnibus ūna omnīs** surripuit Venerēs.

The word order here is difficult, but it is truly effective. The word for "alone" is sandwiched between two forms of "all." The first one hearkens back to "multīs" of line 1. Lesbia is not just pretty to many. No, she surpasses them all. The second form, "omnīs," modifies "Venerēs" and says that she conquers all by stealing the palm in every form of beauty and charm. While he is at it, Catullus has "Venerēs" echo "venustās" above. But by putting "ūna" in between "omnibus" and "omnīs" he is stressing that she alone, of all women, does this single-handedly.

There is no way to translate this artistic arrangement of words gracefully into English. You might even try to do so to prove the point. Only by reading the poem in Latin can you get to know its cleverness and "grain of salt."

Stopping for Some Practice   IRREGULAR LATIN ADJECTIVES

There is no getting around it—the completely irregular comparatives and superlatives must be memorized. This is the case in most languages; just think of "good, better, best" or "many, more, most." Fortunately for the English-speaking Latin student, our language has several words derived from these irregular Latin words, and they can help us memorize the original Latin forms.

Directions: First match the left column with the right column. Then write the Latin word the English word is derived from. Remember that a Latin "i" often ends up in English as a "j." The first one is done as an example.

1.	ameliorate	(D)	_melior_	A.	one who expects the worst
2.	minus	( )	_____	B.	one not yet of legal age
3.	majority	( )	_____	C.	mathematical sign for more
4.	maximize	( )	_____	D.	to make better
5.	minor	( )	_____	E.	to make as large as possible
6.	plus	( )	_____	F.	the smaller part, as in a vote
7.	optimist	( )	_____	G.	mathematical sign for less
8.	pejorative	( )	_____	H.	negative, as in "he said that in a _____ tone"
9.	pessimist	( )	_____	I.	the bigger part, as in a vote
10.	plurality	( )	_____	J.	one who hopes for the best
11.	minority	( )	_____	L.	another word for a majority

Thinking about What You Read

Now go back and compare the two lists you made at the beginning of this chapter with the standards of beauty listed by Catullus. You will want to take a final look at the words he repeats throughout this poem.

Are they fair? How are they like the standards we have today? Are the standards more like people your age or people your parents' age?

Keep This Vocabulary in Mind

If you are going to read Catullus properly, you need to be keyed into some of his most important words having to do with the events and people involved. Below are words from his love poetry and his poetry of friendship.

Directions: Find the synonyms. Match the words on the left with their definitions on the right. Try to do it without using a dictionary; but it is hard, so you may have to use one!

1.	miser	A.	alba
2.	ūror	B.	amīcus
3.	candida	C.	ea quae amāta est
4.	dēliciae	D.	flammātus sum
5.	ardor	E.	ignis amōris
6.	bāsium	F.	neque crūdus nec rudis
7.	labellum	G.	nōn amō
8.	sodālis	H.	nōn laetus
9.	urbānus	I.	osculum
10.	pudīcus	J.	pars faciēī quā bāsia dantur
11.	formōsa	K.	pulcra
12.	ōdī	L.	urbānitās
13.	venustās	M.	verēcundus

CATULLUS 83

LESBIA'S BAD WORDS

BEFORE YOU READ WHAT CATULLUS WROTE

Introduction

Catullus reports that Lesbia speaks badly to him whenever her husband is around. And he says that this makes her husband happy, since he believes this must show that Lesbia hates Catullus.

Catullus has a completely different interpretation of her behavior. He thinks that the fact that she cannot keep quiet about Catullus proves that she has strong feelings for him. She burns (*ūritur*), as he puts it.

Catullus seems to suggest that the opposite of love is not hate, but indifference. Love and hate, both powerful emotions, are closely linked in his mind—if she didn't love him, she would simply ignore him. Try to decide whose interpretation you agree with as you read the poem.

Meter: Elegiac

Keep This Grammar in Mind   MORE CONDITIONS

We have already reviewed future conditions above in Poem 70. Here we deal with others.

Learning about conditions can be made complex or simple. Let's try simple. There are really only two varieties of condition that refer to the present or the past—those that state facts ("factual conditions") and those that state something less real to some degree or other. We call these "contrary to fact conditions" (CTF).

Contrary to Fact Conditions

- state situations that are not true

- and these can be about the **past**, the **present**, or a **mixture** of the two

    | If you **had** seen it, you **would have** enjoyed it. | CTF Past |
    | If you **were** here now, you **would** see what I see. | CTF Present |
    | If you **had** seen it, you **would** be in another state by now. | CTF Mixed |

Factual Conditions

- state true facts

    "If you drop something, gravity makes it fall."
    "If an animal is a mammal, it has warm blood."
    "If you study Latin, you are a superior sort of person."

- Factual conditions are never a problem to translate. Just translate the tenses as you normally would.

Use this chart to help you identify and translate these conditions:

	If Clause	Translation	Main Clause	Translation
CTF Present	Imperfect Subj.	were	Imperfect Subj.	would
CTF Past	Pluperfect Subj.	had	Pluperfect Subj.	would have

Now It's Your Turn   CONDITIONS

Exercise A

Identify the following English sentences as **Contrary to Fact (CTF) Past, Present,** or **Mixed.** Then indicate what tense of the subjunctive the verbs would be in in Latin.

Example:
              plup.   plup.
If you had followed the directions, you would not have gotten lost. **CTF Past**

1. If Caesar had led us, we would have won. _____

2. If Caesar were leading us, we would be winning. _____

3. If you were wise, you would be quiet. _____

4. If I had won the lottery, I would be quite rich now. _____

5. If I were sitting next to Lesbia, I would be unable to speak. _____

Exercise B

Identify the tense and mood of each verb, then tell whether the condition is past, present or mixed. Translate. Use the wordbank (below) to help you with any unfamiliar words.

1. Sī sāna esset, tacēret.

2. Sī tacēret, sāna esset.

3. Sī librum eius lēgissēs, tū quoque eum amārēs.

4. Prope Lesbiam sī ego sedērem, lingua mea torpēret.

5. Sī mihi satis bāsiōrum dedissēs, laetus essem.

6. Nisi tū meās nūgās esse aliquid putārēs, hunc lepidum libellum nōn tibi darem.

7. Sī sōlēs essēmus, occidere et redīre possēmus.

8. Sī puella fūgisset, Catullus secūtus esset.

9. Sī trāns Alpēs trānsīre Catullus vellet, vōs parātī essētis cum eō īre.

10. Sī pecūniam habērem, cēnam tibi optimam darem.

11. Sī linguam ēlegantem illa puella habēret, bella esset.

Wordbank

aliquid something
bāsium, -ī, n. kiss
ēlegāns, -antis (one-termination adj.) elegant
fugiō, -ere, fūgī to flee
lepidus, -a, -um charming
libellus, -ī, m. little book
nūgae, -ārum, f. trifles
occidō, -ere to set
optimus, -a, -um excellent
parātus, -a, -um ready
pecūnia, -ae, f. money
prope prep. + acc. near
redeō, redīre to return, go back
sānus, -a, -um healthy, sane
satis adv. enough
sequor, sequī, secūtus sum to follow
sōl, sōlis, m. sun
torpeō, -ēre to be numb
trāns prep. + acc. across
trānseō, trānsīre to cross

WHAT CATULLUS ACTUALLY WROTE

Vocabulary

1. **praesēns, -entis** (one-termination adj.) present
   plūrimus, -a, -um very many

2. **fatuus, -a, -um** stupid, foolish
   laetitia, -ae, f. happiness

3. **mūlus, -ī,** m. mule
   sentiō, -īre to sense
   oblītus, -a, -um (w. gen.) forgetful

4. **sānus, -a, -um** sane, healthy
   quod because
   ganniō, -īre to snarl
   obloquor, obloquī to contradict

5. **meminī, meminisse** to remember
   ācer, ācris, ācre keen, sharp, fierce

6. **ūrō, -ere** to burn
   loquor, loquī to speak

Notes

1. Pay attention to cases. This line contains a nominative, a dative, an ablative and an accusative.
   praesente virō abl. absolute, "with (her) husband present"

2. **haec** this = the fact that Lesbia does this. **illī** Notice that *illī* has no noun with it, just the adjective *fatuō*. To that foolish (person) = "to that fool."

3. **Mūle** Catullus calls his rival a mule, an animal both stubborn and sterile. Mules were also very good at bearing heavy burdens that people put on them, and Catullus might also be saying, "Silly mule, don't you even feel what we are doing to you?"
   nostrī the genitive of *nōs*. It is common in Latin to use the plural "us" in place of the singular "me." Catullus may mean "me," or he may really mean "us," i.e., "her and me."
   tacēret . . . esset If you forget the type of condition, look back at "Keep This Grammar in Mind."

5. **multō** an ablative with the comparative *ācrior*, "much fiercer." It is easier to translate in this word order: "rēs quae est multō ācrior."

6. **Hoc est** Compare the more common expression, "id est," abbreviated in English i.e., meaning "that is."

As It Was

1   Lesbia mī praesente virō mala plūrima dīcit:

2   haec illī fatuō maxima laetitia est.

3   Mūle, nihil sentīs? Sī nostrī oblīta tacēret,

4   sāna esset. Nunc quod gannit et obloquitur,

5   nōn sōlum meminit, sed, quae multō ācrior est rēs,

6   īrāta est. Hoc est, ūritur et loquitur.

AFTER READING WHAT CATULLUS WROTE

Thinking about How the Author Writes

This poem is about looking beyond the surface of words to understand what they really mean, so let's look deeper than the surface to see what is going on in this poem:

1. Find a word in each of the first three lines that refers to Lesbia's husband. Comment on why Catullus chose them and the order in which he put them.

2. Note that the center of the poem is a Contrary to Fact Condition. What phrase is parallel to *sāna esset* in the "real" version of the situation that Catullus presents? What is parallel to *oblīta*? What is parallel to *tacēret*?

3. Why do you think Catullus inverts the more natural order of the condition, *sī sāna esset, tacēret* to *sī tacēret, sāna esset*?

4. In line 1, Catullus takes apart the normal verb *maledīcere* = to curse, and instead says *mala dīcere* = to say bad things. What do you think of the verbs he chooses in line 4 to describe her speech?

5. Why do you think Catullus ends the poem with verbs that either look or are passive?

Thinking about What You Read

1. In this poem Catullus mixes together facts (e.g., the husband is present) and his own interpretation of those facts (e.g., the husband is a fool). Find other examples.

2. Do you agree with his interpretation of the facts?

3. What qualities do love and hate share?

CATULLUS 85

POET OF THE HEART? POET OF THE HEAD?

BEFORE YOU READ WHAT CATULLUS WROTE

Introduction

You will enjoy this poem for two reasons. The first is the simple fact that it is fairly easy to read. No rearrangement is needed. The words march across the page as if they were written down exactly as Catullus said them. In fact, it is easy to forget, as you read Poem 85, that it is a poem and that Catullus put a great deal of effort into its construction.

The second reason is that in this poem Catullus speaks to us across the centuries in language that seems direct and clear. Anyone who has been in a stormy love relationship will recognize the words and the feelings they represent.

But there is more to the poem than spontaneous outpourings of emotion. We will use this poem, therefore, to show you some of the techniques Catullus uses to create subtle and carefully designed poems that seem to be immediate and direct utterances. When he is acting this way, Catullus has been called the "poet of the heart," whereas other scholars, referring to his Alexandrianism (see introduction to Poem 7) talk of the "poet of the mind." By learning to identify **how** Catullus constructs a poem you will learn that, in fact, the two poets are one man, and that the poet of the heart is never very far from the poet of the head, no matter what poem is being written.

In this poem Catullus explores a feeling that is common to those in love. He burns with love for Lesbia but, due to the way she treats him, he also hates her at times.

Meter: Elegiac

Keep This Grammar in Mind   SOME NOTES ON VERBS—DEPONENTS AND *Fīō*

You may remember that verbs have **tense, voice, and mood.**

- **Tense** refers to words like "present," "future perfect," or "imperfect," and you are familiar with them.

- **Voice** is generally thought of in terms of **active** and **passive**

    Catullus loves Lesbia.   (active)
    Catullus is ignored by Lesbia.   (passive)

- **Mood** includes terms like "indicative," "subjunctive," "infinitive," "imperative," or "participle."

But this poem reminds us that there are also **deponent verbs**, which **look passive but are translated as active verbs**.

How to Recognize Them:

cōnor, cōnārī, cōnātus sum	(1st conjugation) to try
vereor, verērī, veritus sum	(2nd conjugation) to fear
ūtor, ūtī, ūsus sum	(3rd conjugation) to use Note the lost "r" in the infinitive
potior, potīrī, potītus sum	(4th conjugation) to get possession of

- There are only three principal parts
- The principal parts are all passive in form
- The first one ends in -r and the second one in -ī

How to Translate Them:

- First, be sure you are actually dealing with a deponent verb (regular verbs act normally—what looks passive is translated as a passive).

- If you are dealing with a deponent , translate it in the active voice, not the passive.

Example: Using cōnor, -ārī, -ātus sum, to try and excruciō, -āre, -āvī, -ātum, to torture

Deponent		**Regular**	
cōnor	"I try"	excrucior	"I am tortured"
cōnāberis	"you will try"	excruciāberis	"you will be tortured"

Now It's Your Turn   DEPONENTS

Exercise A

These are some deponents used by Catullus. Indicate to which conjugation each verb belongs.

1. abūtor, abūtī, abūsus sum   to use up, abuse   _____
2. adhortor, -ārī, -ātus sum   to urge on   _____
3. adorior, -orīrī, -ortus sum   to start, attack   _____
4. apiscor, apiscī, aptus sum   to obtain, seize   _____
5. dēlābor, dēlābī, dēlapsus sum   to fall, slip   _____
6. experior, -īrī, expertus sum   to try, experience   _____
7. īrascor, īrascī, īrātus sum   to be angry   _____

Exercise B

Using the verbs in Exercise A, translate the forms of the deponent verbs.

1. Ego et tū experīmur. _____
2. Parentēs nōs semper adhortābantur. _____
3. Puellae dēlapsae sunt. _____

4. Lesbia īrāta erat. _____

5. Catilīna! Cūr semper nōs abūteris? _____

6. Catilīna! Quam diū (= how long?) nōs abūtēris? _____

FĪŌ, FIERĪ, FACTUS SUM

The verb **fīō** is a variant on deponents. Look at its principal parts. The first one, which provides the stem for the present, future, and imperfect tenses, is active in form. The next two are passive. It is a **mixed deponent**, sometimes called a **semi-deponent.**

It is a very common verb and can generally be translated by using the English "happen" or "become."

Examples:		
	Quid fit?	What's happening?
	Dīves factus sum!	I became rich!
	Sciō quid factum sit.	I know what happened.
	Multa proelia facta sunt.	Many battles occurred.
	. . . ut semper fit	as always happens

At other times, though, it is better to translate it as a passive:

	Multī impetūs factī sunt.	Many attacks were made.
	Ā Crassō dīves factus sum.	I was made rich by Crassus.
	Sciō quid factum sit.	I know what was done.
	Fiat!	Let it be done!

Use your best judgement as you translate this verb, choosing from "happen," "become," "be made" or "occur."

Pay careful attention to this sort of double sense to the verb as Catullus uses it in Poem 85.

WHAT CATULLUS ACTUALLY WROTE

Vocabulary

1. **ōdī, ōdisse** to hate
    quāre = **cūr**
    fortasse adv. perhaps
    requīrō, requīrere, requīsīvī, requīsītum to ask, inquire about

2. **fīō, fierī, factus sum** to happen, to occur
    sentiō, -īre to sense, feel
    excruciō, -āre to torture

Notes

1. **faciam** By its form, this could be a future . . . but it is not. Why is it subjunctive? Hint: indirect questions are reviewed below.

2. **fierī sentiō** "I feel that it is happening." Check the previous page on the use of this verb.

As It Was

Ōdī et amō. Quāre id faciam, fortasse requīris.

Nesciō, sed fierī sentiō et excrucior.

AFTER READING WHAT CATULLUS WROTE

Thinking about How the Author Writes

As we mentioned above, Catullus seems merely to be pouring out his emotions, as if he were speaking to a friend after a fight with Lesbia. "I love her! But I hate her! How can that be?"

But Catullus is far too great a poet merely to pour out words without thought as to how they appear on the page, even in a two line poem. Look at the poem this way for a moment:

> ŌDĪ et AMŌ. Quārē id FACIAM, fortasse REQUĪRIS.
> NESCIO, sed FIERĪ SENTIŌ et EXCRUCIOR.

- Each line has four verbs

- Of the eight verbs , six are first person singular. There is no doubt about who is the focal point of this poem.

- Most of the verbs are active (*ōdī, amō, faciam, requīris, nesciō, sentiō*), stressing that Catullus is doing something. But the poem ends with the only true passive in the poem, *excrucior*, stressing that something is being done to him. Is this not just how a wronged lover feels?

- Finally, notice *fierī*, the present deponent infinitive of the verb *fiō*. It can mean, equally, "it is being done" or "it is happening." Its ambivalence as a semi-deponent shows up perfectly here, highlighting Catullus' own ambivalence.

The poet of the head is never far from the poet of the heart.

Stopping for Some Practice   INDIRECT QUESTIONS AND SEQUENCE OF TENSES

- A **direct question** is in the indicative.

    Quid facis?   What are you doing?
    Cūr id fēcistī? Why did you do that?

- But remember that **indirect questions** are always in the subjunctive. They tend to follow a formula.

Indirect Questions

IQ = a "verb of the head" + a question word + a verb in the subjunctive

   "Verbs of the head" are verbs of thinking or sensing, e.g. "reckon," "see," "hear," "guess," "know," "find out."

Examples:
Direct:	Quid facis?	What are you doing?
Indirect:	Sciō quid faciās.	I know what are you doing.
Direct:	Cūr id fecistī?	Why did you do that?
Indirect:	Sciō cūr id fēcerīs.	I know why you did that.

And from this poem

Fortasse requīris quārē id faciam.   Perhaps you ask why I do this.

Is this Direct Question or Indirect Question?

Which Subjunctive? The Sequence of Tenses

Indirect Question is a great opportunity to review the Sequence of Tenses and how to translate the various tenses of the subjunctive in dependent clauses.

Primary Sequence	Translation	Time Shown by Subjunctive
Sciō quid faciās.	I know what you are doing.	Same time as main verb
Sciō quid fēcerīs.	I know what you did.	Time before the main verb
Sciō quid factūrus sīs.	I know what you are going to do.	Time after the main verb
Secondary Sequence	**Translation**	**Time Shown by Subjunctive**
Scīvī quid facerēs.	I knew what you were doing.	Same time as main verb
Scīvī quid fēcissēs.	I knew what you had done.	Time before the main verb
Scīvī quid factūrus essēs.	I knew what you were going to do.	Time after the main verb

Exercise C

Translate these sentences to show that you can deal with the sequence of tenses and how it affects meaning.

Example:

Catullus sē rogat cūr Lesbia alium virum amet.
   Catullus asks himself why Lesbia loves another man.

Catullus sē rogat cūr Lesbia alium virum amāverit.
   Catullus asks himself why Lesbia loved another man.

1. Catullus sē rogat cūr Lesbia alium virum amātūra sit.

2. Catullus semper sē rogābat cūr Lesbia alium virum amāret.

3. Catullus sē rogāvit cūr Lesbia alium virum amāret.

4. Catullus sē rogāvit cūr Lesbia alium virum amāvisset.

5. Catullus sē rogāvit cūr Lesbia alium virum amātūra esset.

Keep This Vocabulary in Mind

Exercise D

All the following English words are all derived from the Latin words Catullus uses in this short poem. First find the appropriate Latin word in the poem. Then write out a definition for each English word. Then use five of them in a sentence that demonstrates the meaning of the word. For example, do not just say, "She was pleasant," but "Since she was nice to everyone, most people thought she was pleasant."

1. excruciating
2. fiat (not the car!)
3. odious
4. odium
5. requisite
6. requisition
7. sensible
8. sentient
9. unrequited

CATULLUS 43

A Girl with Several Shortcomings

Before You Read What Catullus Wrote

Introduction

Catullus never actually tells us what Lesbia looks like. In this poem he gives some hints by enumerating some attractive qualities another woman lacks and expressing amazement that anyone would compare her with Lesbia.

Meter: Hendecasyllabic

Things to Consider before You Read

1. What physical characteristics make someone attractive?

2. What other characteristics make someone attractive?

3. Is the answer to number two the same for a boy and a girl?

WHAT CATULLUS ACTUALLY WROTE

Vocabulary	Notes

1. **minimus, -a, -um** very small
   nāsus, -ī, m. nose

2. **pēs, pedis,** m. foot
   niger, -gra, -grum black, dark

3. **digitus, -ī,** m. finger
   siccus, -a, -um dry

4. **sānē** adv. clearly
   nimis adv. too, very
   ēlegāns, -antis (one-termination adj.) elegant
   lingua, -ae, f. tongue

5. **dēcoctor, -ōris,** m. squanderer, bankrupt
   amīca, -ae, f. mistress
   Formiānus, -a, -um Formian = from Formiae, an
   Italian town

6. **prōvincia, -ae,** f. province
   nārrō, -āre to tell

7. **comparō, -āre** to compare

8. **saeclum, -ī,** n. age, era
   īnsipiēns, -entis (one-termination adj.) unwise
   infacētus, -a, -um witless

---

1. **minimō . . . nāsō** abl. of description. There are several of these in the first four lines. A simple "with" will do nicely for a translation.

2. **ocellīs** diminutive from *oculus*.

5. **Dēcoctōris . . . Formiānī** "The bankrupt from Formiae" was a man named Mamurra, a lieutenant of Caesar's in Gaul known for his lavish lifestyle.

6. **tēn** = **tēne.** The *-ne* indicates a question. *Tē* is the accusative subject of *esse* in indirect statement.
   prōvinicia: Of course the province as such is not talking and this is a clever device called "metonymy" that we have met above and will return to below. Apart from this, what does Catullus hint at by stressing the girl does not live in Rome?

As It Was

1 Salvē, nec minimō puella nāsō

2 nec bellō pede nec nigrīs ocellīs

3 nec longīs digitīs nec ōre siccō

4 nec sānē nimis ēlegante linguā,

5 dēcoctōris amīca Formiānī.

6 Tēn prōvincia narrat esse bellam?

7 Tēcum Lesbia nostra comparātur?

8 Ō saeclum īnsapiēns et infacētum!

AFTER READING WHAT CATULLUS WROTE

Thinking about How the Author Writes

1. Count the number of negative words in the poem. Why does Catullus use so many negatives?

2. What purpose do the words *sānē nimis* in line 4 serve?

3. Catullus refers to the woman in this poem by her appearance, by her manner of speech and by the company she keeps. Why do you think he does this? Why does he not give the girl a name?

4. What word is emphasized in lines 6 and 7? How?

5. If this poem is about what makes a woman attractive, why does Catullus end with an exclamation about the folly of the present day?

Thinking about What You Read

The Catullan Canon of Beauty and the Vocabulary of Love

This poem surely gives us a view of what makes a woman beautiful to Catullus and his friends. By listing negative traits Catullus makes it pretty clear what positive traits this girl lacks. Going back to the poem, now, make a list of the positive traits that Catullus and his friends would find attractive in a woman.

Now answer these questions:

1. Catullus talks about Lesbia only indirectly in this poem, but he still tells us a lot. What do we learn about Lesbia and why Catullus finds her attractive?

2. Compare the *puella* in this poem to Quintia from Poem 86.

CATULLUS 13

An Invitation

Before You Read What Catullus Wrote

Introduction

In this poem, Catullus invites his friend Fabullus to dinner. It is an unusual invitation, however, as Catullus attaches several conditions. Fabullus is asked to bring the dinner, the company (a pretty girl), the wine, the wit and the laughter. Catullus assures Fabullus that he will make it worth his while by giving in exchange a special perfume—true love.

Meter: Hendecasyllabic

Keep This Grammar in Mind   Condition Review

We have already reviewed conditions above in Poems 70 and 83. Go back if you need to and then do the following exercise.

Now It's Your Turn

Exercise A

Identify the tense and mood of all the verbs. Identify the type of condition and translate:

1. Sī mihi multa bāsia **dederis**, laetus **erō**.

2. Nisi tū meās nūgās esse aliquid **putāvissēs**, illum lepidum libellum nōn tibi **dedissem**.

3. Sī sōl **occidisset**, nunc nox **esset**. (a "mixed" condition)

4. Sī causam **quaesīvissēs**, nihil **locūtus essem**.

5. Sī Lesbia **fugiat**, Catullus **sequātur**.

6. Sī librum eius **legēs**, eum **amābis**.

7. Sī aliquid **accidisset**, māter sē **culpāvisset**.

8. Sī illud unguentum **olfēcissēs**, id emere **voluissēs**.

9. Sī Catullus sānus **esset**, Lesbiam amāre **dēsineret**.

10. Haec sī **attuleris**, unguentum **dabō**.

WHAT CATULLUS ACTUALLY WROTE

Vocabulary	Notes

Vocabulary

1. **cēnō, -āre** to dine
   apud prep. + acc. at the house of

2. **paucī, -ae, -a** few
   faveō, -ēre (w. dat.) to favor

3. **afferō, afferre, attulī, allātum** to bring along

5. **vīnum, -ī,** n. wine
   sāl, salis, m. salt, wit
   cachinnus, -ī, m. laughter

6. **venustus, -a, -um** attractive

8. **plēnus, -a, -um** full
   sacculus, -ī, m. little bag, purse
   arānea, -ae, f. cobweb

9. **contrā** adv. in return
   accipiō, -ere to receive
   merus, -a, -um pure

10. **seu** conj. or if
    suāvis, -e pleasant, agreeable
    ēlegāns, -antis (one-termination adj.) elegant
    ve conj. or

11. **unguentum, -ī,** n. perfume

12. **dōnō, -āre, -āvī, -ātum** to give
    Venus, Veneris, f. Venus
    Cupīdō, Cupīdinis, m. Cupid

13. **olfaciō, -ere** to smell
    rogō, -āre to ask

14. **nāsus, -ī,** m. nose

Notes

2. **dī = deī**

3. **attuleris** What tense and mood? Hint: it is in a condition that we reviewed at Poem 70.

4. **nōn sine** an elegant understatement in place of the obvious *cum*. This type of double negative is called litotes.

6. **Haec** Neut. acc. pl., referring to all the things mentioned in lines 3–5. "These things."
   venuste noster two adjectives in the vocative. "Our attractive fellow" sounds wrong in English. What would sound more natural? Remember that "venustus" can mean "charming."

7. **tuī Catullī** Try translating in this word order: *sacculus tuī Catullī est plēnus arāneārum.*

10. **quid = aliquid** "anything."
    suāvius ēlegantius What form are these adjectives? See Keep This Grammar in Mind 72, above, and be sure to translate them accordingly.

12. **dōnārunt** What form is this verb? Do you remember the term "syncopated?" See Poem 8 if you need a reminder.
    Venerēs Cupīdinēsque The plurals here add to the extravagant playfulness of the poem

13. **cum olfaciēs** Latin uses the future tense to refer to the future. In English, because it is a subordinate clause, we use the present tense: "when you smell."

As It Was

1   Cēnābis bene, mī Fabulle, apud mē

2   paucīs, sī tibi dī favent, diēbus,

3   sī tēcum attuleris bonam atque magnam

4   cēnam, nōn sine candidā puellā

5   et vīnō et sale et omnibus cachinnīs.

6   Haec sī, inquam, attuleris, venuste noster,

7   cēnābis bene, nam tuī Catullī

8   plēnus sacculus est arāneārum.

9   Sed contrā accipiēs merōs amōrēs

10   seu quid suāvius ēlegantiusve est:

11   nam unguentum dabo quod meae puellae

12   dōnārunt Venerēs Cupīdinēsque,

13   quod tū cum olfaciēs, deōs rogābis

14   tōtum ut tē faciant, Fabulle, nāsum.

AFTER READING WHAT CATULLUS WROTE

Thinking about How the Author Writes

Notice how this poem gradually becomes more and more absurd. The clues are in the words themselves. A careful look at the words will help you understand the movement of the poem.

1. The poem begins with a promise of dinner. Then Catullus puts the promised dinner off for a few days with an ablative phrase. What is this phrase? (Latin and English)

2. Then he interrupts that phrase with a condition that seems nothing more than a throwaway line like "God willing." What is this condition? (Latin and English)

3. But then the requirements for coming to dinner become more and more onerous. For example, what else must Fabullus supply to this dinner party? (English only)

4. Then Catullus shows off for his friend by sneaking his own name into the poem. Read line 3 with poetic elision: *sī tēc' attuleris bon' atque magnam.* Where do you hear Catullus' name in this line?

5. Do the same for line 6: *Haec s', inqu', attuleris, venuste noster.* Where did he hide it here?

6. What effect does Catullus create by making *nāsum* the last word of the poem? Seriousness? Sadness? Certainly not. What is he after?

CATULLUS 50

ABOUT LAST NIGHT

BEFORE YOU READ WHAT CATULLUS WROTE

Introduction

Catullus addresses this poem to his close friend Licinius Calvus. The two had spent the previous evening drinking and exchanging clever bits of poetic improvisation. In the poem, Catullus uses the language of a hopeless lover, wittily expressing how strongly he is affected by Calvus' charm. Since the poetry of unrequited love is stock fare for their Neoteric circle, Calvus would certainly understand the poem as a learned and charming thanks for a pleasant evening and a hope that they will see more of each other soon. Catullus ends the poem with a mock tragic note, threatening Calvus with divine retribution if he spurns his request.

Meter: Hendecasyllabic

Keep This Grammar in Mind   PARTICIPLES

Form and Use

We took a quick look at participles above in Poem 1. You will recall that a participle is part verb, part adjective. They are more common in Latin than in English, and sometimes act more like a verb, sometimes more like an adjective. When Catullus (in Poem 45) calls India *India tosta*, the participle functions like a simple adjective, "parched" = "dry." But when he describes himself (in Poem 44) as *refectus* in the line *refectus maximās tibi grātēs agō*, we can translate the one word with a whole clause: "(Now that I have been) refreshed, I give you very great thanks."

Participles are more common in Latin because they can be used in so many ways. Consider the following sentence from a long Catullan poem:

A   B   B   A

Theseus discessit **irrita prōmissa linquēns**.   Theseus departed leaving promises unfulfilled.

This sentence shows the variety of uses to which participles can be put in Latin.

- *Linquēns* is a **present active participle** and has a simple verbal translation: "leaving."

- *Prōmissa* is a **perfect passive participle** used as a noun: "things having been promised" = "promises."

- *Irrita* is a **perfect passive participle** made negative (*ratus* becomes *irritus*) and used as an adjective: "unfulfilled."

Thus, within one sentence we have three participles—one verb-like, one adjective-like, one noun-like.

Perfect Infinitive

Because *esse* is often left out in Latin, the perfect participle can also stand in for the perfect infinitive. For this reason the participle can often be translated as part of an indirect statement.

Mē dolōre **cōnfectum** vidēs.   You see **me worn out** by grief.

or

You see **that I am worn out** by grief.

Now It's Your Turn

Exercise A

The quotes below are all from Catullus himself. We have highlighted the participles so they are easy to find. Identify their tense and voice and then translate the sentences. Refer back to the discussion in Poem 1 or in the Grammar Section at the end of this book (p. 150) if you need some help. Use the wordbank (below) to help you with any unfamiliar words.

1. **Circumsiliēns** hūc illūc passer ad dominam pīpiābat.

    Type: Present Active
    Trans.:   "Leaping about here and there the sparrow used to chirp at its mistress."

2. Flōs cecidit arātrō **praetereunte tactus**.

3. **Sedēns** adversus Lesbiam **rīdentem** spectat.

4. Ariadnē patrem relīquit, iuvenem sanguine Minotaurī **rēspersum secūta**.

5. Tibi libellum pūmice **expolītum** dōnō.

6. Nōn **inmerentī** tibi hunc dōnō.

7. Multōs virōs **complexa**, nūllōs vērē amat.

8. Ad tē, frāter, adveniō per multa aequora **vectus**.

9. Illinc abiī tuō lepōre **incēnsus**.

10. Tōtō in lectō versābar, **cupiēns** vidēre lūcem.

Wordbank

abeō, abīre, abiī to go away

adveniō, -īre to come to

adversus prep. + acc. opposite

aequor, -ōris, n. sea

arātrum, -ī, n. plow

Ariadnē, -ēs, f. Ariadne, Cretan princess who helped Theseus kill the Minotaur

cadō -ere, cecidī, cāsum to fall

circumsiliō, -īre to jump around

complector, -ī, complexus sum to embrace

cupiō, -ere to desire

dōnō, -āre to give

expoliō, -īre, -īvī, -ītum to polish

flōs, flōris, m. flower

illinc adv. from there

incendō, -ere, incendī, incēnsum to inflame

iuvenis, -is, m. young man

lectus, -ī, m. bed

lepos, lepōris, m. charm

libellus, -ī, m. little book

lux, lūcis, f. light

mereō, -ēre to deserve

Minotaurus, -ī, m. the Minotaur, a half-human monster killed by Theseus

passer, passeris, m. sparrow

pīpiō, -āre to chirp

praetereō, -īre (present participle stem: *praetereunt-*) to pass

pūmex, -icis, f. pumice stone

relinquō, -ere, relīquī, relictum to leave

rēspergō, -ere, rēspersī, rēspersum to spatter

rīdeō, -ēre to laugh

sanguō, -inis, m. blood

sequor, sequī, secūtus sum to follow

tangō, -ere, tetigī, tactum to touch

vehō, -ere, vexī, vectum to carry

versō, -āre to turn

WHAT CATULLUS ACTUALLY WROTE

Vocabulary

1. **ōtiōsus, -a, -um** at leisure

2. **lūdō, -ere, lūsī, lūsum** to play
   tabella, -ae, f. writing tablet, notebook

3. **dēlicātus, -a, -um** luxurious, self-indulgent

4. **versiculus, -ī**, m. little verse
   uterque, utraque, utrumque each

5. **numerus, -ī**, m. meter

6. **reddō, -ere** to give back, exchange
   mūtuus, -a, -um shared, reciprocal
   iocus, -ī, m. joke, jest
   vīnum, -ī, n. wine

7. **illinc** adv. from there
   abeō, abīre, abiī to go away
   lepos, lepōris, m. charm

8. **incendō, -ere, incendī, incēnsum** to inflame
   facētiae, -ārum, f. pl. wit

9. **cibus, -ī**, m. food
   iuvō, -āre to help

10. **somnus, -ī**, m. sleep
    tegō, -ere to cover
    quiēs, quiētis, f. rest

11. **indomitus, -a, -um** uncontrollable
    furor, -ōris, m. madness

12. **versō, -āre** to keep turning
    cupiō, -ere to desire
    lux, lūcis, f. light

13. **loquor, loquī, locūtus sum** to speak

Notes

1. **Hesternō . . . diē** "yester . . . day."
   Licinī Gaius Licinius Calvus was a member of Catullus' circle of Neoteric poets.

3. **convēnerat** It makes sense to translate this impersonal verb with a first person subject: "It had been agreed" = "we had agreed." *Ut* plus the indicative generally is translated as "as."

4. **nostrum** genitive of *nōs* with *uterque*: "each of us."

5. **illōc** = **illō**, abl. with a *-c* making it parallel to *hōc*. Both adjectives modify *numerō*. The two poets were exchanging witty remarks in various meters.

6. **reddēns mūtua** "exchanging witty remarks back and forth."

9. **ut nec** This is a sort of result clause—"I left **so** stirred up, that . . . " The normal negative of a result clause is "ut non." What is the effect of "ut nec . . . nec"?

10. **ocellōs** diminutive of *oculus*. The symptoms Catullus describes in these lines are characteristic of the unrequited lover.

11. Note the stranded adjective **tōtō**. What noun do you think it modifies?
    indomitus furōre "wild with frenzy" *furor* is the typical state of the lover.

As It Was

1 Hesternō Licinī diē otiōsī

2 multum lūsimus in meīs tabellīs,

3 ut convēnerat esse dēlicātōs.

4 Scrībēns versiculōs uterque nostrum

5 lūdēbat numerō modo hōc modo illōc

6 reddēns mutua per iocum atque vīnum.

7 Atque illinc abiī tuō lepōre

8 incēnsus, Licinī, facētiīsque,

9 ut nec mē miserum cibus iuvāret

10 nec somnus tegeret quiēte ocellōs,

11 sed tōtō indomitus furōre lectō

12 versārer cupiēns vidēre lūcem

13 ut tēcum loquerer, simulque ut essem.

Vocabulary

14. **dēfessus, -a, -um** tired
    labor, -ōris, m. labor, suffering
    membrum, -ī, n. limb
    postquam conj. after

15. **sēmimortuus, -a, -um** half-dead
    lectulus, -ī, m. little bed
    iaceō, -ēre to lie

16. **iūcundus, -a, -um** agreeable, delightful
    poēma, poēmatis, n. poem

17. **perspiciō, -ere** to perceive
    dolor, -ōris, m. grief, sadness

18. **audāx, audācis** bold, rash
    prex, precis, f. prayer

19. **ōrō, -āre** to pray, beg
    dēspuō, -ere to scorn, spurn

20. **poena, -ae,** f. punishment
    Nemesis, -is, f. Nemesis, goddess of retribution
    reposcō, -ere to demand, exact

21. **vēmēns, -entis** (one-termination adj.) violent
    laedō, -ere to harm

Notes

14. Try translating in this word order: *At postquam (mea) membra, dēfessa labōre, iacēbant sēmimortua in (meō) lectulō, . . .*

17. **ex quō = ut,** another way to introduce a purpose clause, using the relative pronoun to link it more closely to the *poēma* in the main clause. It was conventional for an unrequited lover to write a poem to communicate his feelings to his beloved.

18. **cave sīs** beware of being = "don't be."

19. **ocelle** The diminutive of *oculus* is used as a term of endearment: "darling."

20. **nē** Purpose or result clause?

21. **cavētō laedere** The ending *-tō* marks this form as a "future imperative," and as such stresses that Licinius should continue to be careful for some time to come.

As It Was (CONTINUED)

14   At dēfessa labōre membra postquam

15   sēmimortua lectulō iacēbant

16   hoc, iucunde, tibī poēma fēcī,

17   ex quō perspicerēs meum dolōrem.

18   Nunc audāx cave sīs, precēsque nostrās

19   ōrāmus, cave dēspuās, ocelle,

20   nē poenās Nemesis reposcat ā tē.

21   Est vēmēns dea; laedere hanc cavētō.

AFTER READING WHAT CATULLUS WROTE

Thinking about How the Author Writes   WORD SPECIFICS

1. What words in the first three lines of this poem establish the mood for the scene?

2. Leisure (*otium*) is also mentioned in Poem 51. Take another look at its use there before going on.

3. Find examples of language Catullus uses in this poem that is typical of a lover. Does *otium* have anything to do with it?

Thinking about What You Read

1. How might you respond if you had just had a great time with a friend of yours?

2. How is Catullus' response to his evening typical of what you have seen of him?

CATULLUS 101

FAREWELL TO HIS BROTHER

BEFORE YOU READ WHAT CATULLUS WROTE

Introduction

We know virtually nothing about Catullus other than what he tells us in his poems. We know that he served a time on the staff of a very unpopular governor in Bithynia, far from Rome, and that he really did not enjoy his stay. And in Poem 65 (below, Part II) we learn that Catullus had a brother who died. In this poem we learn that the brother died in Bithynia and Catullus is in the province at his brother's grave site. The death of one so young certainly became a major theme for Catullus.

The poem is both familiar and distant to us as we read it today. Most of us have had some sense of death, perhaps, unfortunately, of a close family member. But few of us have had to travel a great distance to the funeral. And things then were very different from things today.

For example, Catullus had no way to rush to his brother's side before he died. Bithynia lies about 800 miles from Rome (see map, front of book). And once he found out his brother was dead, it may have taken him the better part of a week to travel there—first making his way to the Roman port of Ostia, then by a fairly slow ship to that very strange and very distant part of the world and then, by land again, to the grave site.

Today we commonly have wakes where the body of the dead person is on view and we can gradually get used to the fact that he or she is gone. In cultures where the body is buried the same day, there still is a formal period of mourning where friends and relatives come to the house and mourn the passing of the loved one.

None of this for Catullus. When he finally arrived at the grave site there was no body to view since his brother was cremated. There was no crowd of fellow mourners since the poem implies that he made the journey alone. He would have performed the expected rites and would have made offerings of wine, milk, honey or flowers. But what to say? He had many days aboard ship to think about what he would say to his brother when he finally arrived.

Before you read, you will benefit from taking a quiet moment and thinking what you might say. What emotions would you have if you had not seen this person for a long time and had traveled halfway around the known world just to stand at his or her grave in a foreign land? Think what your last words might be and then, and only then, go on to see what Catullus' answer to this very human experience was.

Meter: Elegiac

WHAT CATULLUS ACTUALLY WROTE

Vocabulary

1. **gēns, gentis,** f. nation
    aequor, aequoris, n. sea
    vehō, vehere, vexī, vectum to carry

2. **īnferiae, īnferiārum,** f. pl. funeral rites

3. **postrēmus, -a, -um** last, final
    dōnō, dōnāre, dōnāvī, dōnātum to give, to make a dedication to someone

4. **mūtus, -a, -um** silent, mute
    nēquīquam adv. in vain
    alloquor, alloquī, allocūtus sum to speak to, address

5. **quandōquidem** conj. since, because
    auferō, auferre, abstulī, ablātum take away

6. **indignē** adv. undeservedly
    adimō, adimere, -ēmī, -ēmptum to take away, snatch away

7. **prīscus, -a, -um** ancient, time-honored
    mōs, mōris, m. custom, manner

8. **trādō, -ere, -didī, -ditum** to hand over, pass along or down
    tristis, triste sad

9. **accipiō, -ere, -cēpī, -ceptum** to accept, receive, take
    fraternus, -a, -um brotherly, a brother's
    mānō, -āre, -āvī, -ātum to drip
    flētus, -ūs, m. weeping, tears

10. **perpetuus, -a, -um** eternal

Notes

2. Rites for the dead included offerings of wine, milk, honey, and flowers.

6. **Frāter** is not nominative. He is being directly addressed. What case, therefore? Once you have that, you know the case that *adēmpte* is in. Remember that it is a passive participle. His brother has been snatched away.

    mihi How to explain this dative? There are many names the grammars have given it—dative of interest (the one interested in the action of the verb), dative of disadvantage (obviously Catullus is disadvantaged by his brother's death), dative of reference. More crucial is that you sense the intensely personal nature of the word. This poem is about the brother to be sure—but it is equally about Catullus.

10. **Perpetuum** is used here as a noun. So what might "in perpetuum" mean?

As It Was

1   Multās per gentēs et multa per aequora vectus

2   adveniō hās miserās, frāter, ad īnferiās,

3   ut tē postremō dōnārem mūnere mortis

4   et mūtam nēquīquam alloquerer cinerem.

5   Quandōquidem fortūna mihi tētē abstulit ipsum,

6   heu miser indignē frāter adēmpte mihi,

7   nunc tamen intereā haec, prīscō quae mōre parentum

8   trādita sunt tristī mūnere ad īnferiās,

9   accipe frāternō multum mānantia flētū,

10   atque in perpetuum, frāter, avē atque valē.

AFTER READING WHAT CATULLUS WROTE

Thinking about How the Author Writes   ANALYZING A POEM

The emotion here is right on the surface. We can see Catullus standing at the grave and saying these very words. But the poet is never far away and in this poem we can see Catullus using several bits of poetic craft to make the emotion all the more telling. We have reprinted the poem on the next page with questions to help you analyze it.

Pronouns as Structure

- First, in the poem below, circle every use of a personal pronoun.

- Which pronouns predominate? What does that tell you about the poem and its focus?

- Catullus has been very careful to put the pronouns in careful juxtaposition. How does this help further the emotional content of the poem?

Alliteration

Alliteration is most commonly defined as the purposeful repetition of consonant sounds. You may well have noticed the predominance of the "m" sound in the poem. Underline every "m" in the poem below, noting especially where they occur next to each other.

That there are so many of them and that they come next to each other is no accident. What sound might it be meant to imitate? Remember the setting.

Word Choice

To be a poet is to choose, and especially to choose among words. For example, Catullus chose, in line 7, to use "parentum." It is not literally true that these are the rites of "our parents." They are the rites of all of Rome's ancestors. But by using "parens," Catullus reminds us that he is addressing his brother.

Likewise, there are many word repetitions in this poem. Sometimes whole words are repeated and sometimes related words (e.g., *frāter* and *frāternus*). Go to the poem again and find groups of repetitions. Remember, Catullus did this on purpose. What do you think he had in mind?

Word Order

Since we read left to right, the word at the end of a line or a phrase has a special impact once we get there, often serving to put the rest of the line in focus. Let's look at an example.

This simple line *adveniō hās miserās, frāter, ad īnferiās,* is carefully constructed so that the important word comes last. Consider its literal translation, "I come to these sad, brother, funeral rites." As we go through the line we first get to "these," a neutral word. "Sad" gives us some hint, but "funeral rites" is reserved for last place in the line and once we get there the entire rest of the line is suddenly, and sadly, clear.

Go through the poem one last time, now, and notice the words that end lines. Are they more full of impact because of their position? Do they help raise the emotional content of the poem?

1   Multās per gentēs et multa per aequora vectus

2   adveniō hās miserās, frāter, ad īnferiās,

3   ut tē postremō dōnārem mūnere mortis

4   et mūtam nēquīquam alloquerer cinerem.

5   Quandōquidem fortūna mihi tētē abstulit ipsum,

6   heu miser indignē frāter adēmpte mihi,

7   nunc tamen intereā haec, prīscō quae mōre parentum

8   trādita sunt tristī mūnere ad īnferiās,

9   accipe frāternō multum mānantia flētū,

10   atque in perpetuum, frāter, avē atque valē.

PART II

THE LONG POEMS

Introduction

The poems in Part I are the most popular and most commonly read of Catullus' work. They are short, fairly straightforward, and deal with the universal themes of love and friendship.

In Part II we introduce you to his longer and more complex poems. In these poems the poet of the heart recedes into the background and the poet of the head takes center stage. These poems require a bit more work to understand, but they are as much a part of Catullus' world as the poems of love and friendship are.

Because the poems are written in a more obviously literary style, we offer you assistance with a rewrite of Poem 64 and font help for both poems.

CATULLUS 64.1–15

EPYLLION ON JASON AND MEDEA

BEFORE YOU READ WHAT CATULLUS WROTE

A Note on Meter

The meter is dactylic hexameter, the meter traditionally associated with epic. Since you have already learned the elegiac meter, you already know the dactylic hexameter since it is used as the first line of every elegiac couplet.

Catullus and the Alexandrians

In this poem you meet, undiluted, the other Catullus you have briefly encountered in other poems—the so-called "Catullus of the head." In his love and friendship poetry Catullus certainly uses a lot of poetic craft—word order, clever word repetition, alliteration, and more. But in those poems he is at pains to push this craft to the background so that the emotions and feelings have the front of the stage, and the handicraft of making poetry is in the background, necessary and useful, but not visible.

Catullus wrote several other poems, however, where he **wanted** his readers to see and admire his craft, especially his learning and erudition. He wants to show off his knowledge of mythology, for example, and his ability to write in the meters of epic. One important reason for this was that his group of friends and fellow poets, the "New Poets" (*poētae novī* or *neotericī*), held as a common value that this sort of learning was important. In doing this they were reacting to a movement that had preceded them, called the **Alexandrian Movement**.

After the death of Alexander the Great in 323 BC, one of his generals, Ptolemy, had established an enormous library and learning center in Alexandria, Egypt. One goal of the library was to have an error-free copy of every bit of Greek literature that had been written up to that date. You must remember that in an era when manuscripts were copied by hand, a lot of mistakes would creep into manuscripts. So, once accurate copies of the works were available, scholars and poets alike came to Alexandria to study the works. The results were probably predictable.

The scholar-poets first decided that it was no longer possible to write huge epics like those of Homer. They promoted instead a form called the *epyllion*, a mini-epic that would tell a smaller tale on a smaller scale. It would still be in dactylic hexameter verse, the verse of epic, however. The most famous Alexandrian poet who practiced and promoted this style was called Callimachus and he proclaimed "*mega biblion, mega kakon,*" or, "big book, big evil." The pithy phrase won approval and soon any poet who wanted to be thought worthy of the name was writing an *epyllion*.

But poets love to embellish and to leave their imprint on their material. If they could not write on an epic scale and could not change the meter, they would change the embellishment. That is to say they would pay more attention to the small details of the mini-epic and would find new ways of saying things and many of these ways would entail showing off the erudition that befitted a poet-scholar of Alexandria.

To be honest, this style does not suit our modern tastes very readily. Listen to a translation—a very literal translation—of the first three lines of Catullus 64.

Once, pine trees born on the Peliac apex
Are said to have swum through the liquid waves of Neptune
toward the Aeetean waves and to the borders of Phasis.

This is not the sort of thing that comes naturally to us. After all, what it really says, in plain Latin, is "Once, a ship made of pine trees in Thessaly sailed over the sea to Colchis." But to know this you have to know that Pelion is a mountain in Thessaly, that Aeetes was king of Colchis and Medea's father, and that the Phasis was a major river in Colchis.

Once you know that you immediately say, "Oh yes, the story of the Golden Fleece!"

Why write this way? It is hard to give a definitive answer. All we can say is that the authors of Catullus' day thought there was great merit in this sort of writing and that many other authors wrote *epyllia*. And if you really want to know Catullus, you have to acknowledge and understand both sides of him. You would not have lasted long in his circle of friends if you did not "get" his learned allusions. Remember that the women to whom these poets wrote love poetry were expected to have that spark of wit and intelligence that made them worthy to associate with the new poets, the "in crowd." We, as readers, owe him the same.

In what follows, then, we will attempt to give you, a modern reader, enough information to follow the allusions Catullus drops. We will give you this **before** you read a passage—not as you read it or after you read it in the form of a footnote. After all, Catullus' audience had most of the knowledge before they read—you should also.

Now It's Your Turn   ALEXANDRIAN ALLUSION

Exercise A

Before you read you should have a bit more practice in this Alexandrian, allusional style. Try to identify the following figures from antiquity. The answers appear at the end of this section on Poem 64.

1. The god who limps

2. The ox-eyed wife of Zeus

3. The stealer of fire

Now try these, more indirect allusions from our own culture. See how many you "get" before checking the answers.

4. The Tennessean hero of Texas

5. He of the Blue Ox

6. He of the wooden teeth

7. Whale-devoured child of Gepetto

8. Son of Jor-El

9. Parter of waters

10. The Texas-slain president

11. Master of Alfred

12. Master of Baker Street

13. Master of Graceland

Exercise B

Think about the sorts of people and things that you know from your everyday culture (superheroes, media stars) and make a list of "Alexandrian" allusions for them. You might work in teams and try them out on your classmates in a sort of contest.

NOTES

HELPING YOU TO READ WHAT CATULLUS WROTE

This is the first of several small rewrites of Catullus' original words. First try reading the poem in these sections and then move directly to the unchanged form.

Vocabulary

1. **pīnus, -ūs**, f. pine tree (most tree names are feminine gender)
   prognātus, -a, -um lit., "born"
   vertex, -icis, m. top, apex
   Pēliacus, -a, -um an adjective referring to Mt. Pelion and modifying *vertice*.

2. **nō, nāre** to swim, float
   liquidus, -a, -um clear, liquid

3. **fluctus, -ūs**, m. wave
   fīnis, -is, m. end. In plural, "boundary, territory"
   Aeētēus, -a, -um of King Aeetes
   Phāsis, -idos, m. the river Phasis, in Cholcis. See map at beginning of the book.

4. **lectus, -a, -um** chosen
   rōbur, -oris, n. oak
   pūbēs, -is, f. youth

5. **āvertō, āvertere, āvertī, āversum** to remove, take away
   aurātus, -a, -um covered in gold
   pellis, -is, f. skin, pelt
   optō, -āre to wish, desire

6. **vadum, -ī**, n. a shoal, in the plural, "ocean"
   salsus, -a, -um salted, salty
   citus, -a, -um swift
   puppis, -is, f. the stern of a boat. By metonymy, a frequent poetic word for boat.
   dēcurrō, -currere, -currī, -cursum to run, speed
   audeō, audēre, ausus sum to dare

7. **caerulus, -a, -um** blue (more commonly "caeruleus")
   aequor, -oris, n. "the flat place," a common poetic word for the ocean.
   abiegnus, -a, -um made from the **abiēs** tree; fir, pine
   verro, -ere, verrī, versum to sweep
   palma, -ae, f. the palm of the hand. What part of an oar is meant?

Notes

1. **pīnus ... nasse** Pine trees obviously do not sail to Cholcis. They have to be converted into ships first and even then ships do not actually swim. A good example of Alexandrianism with metonymy (a part for the whole) and then personification (giving human qualities to an inanimate object)
   Pēliācō Mt. Pelion was a mountain in Thessaly, Jason's home land.

2. **dīcuntur** as commonly, introducing an indirect statement
   nāsse syncopated form for **nāvisse**

3. **Aeētēs**: the king of Colchis and Medea's father

4. **cum** simply, "when"
   robora: a metaphor, but not a terribly hard one to follow. These select youth are so strong that they are the "oaks" of the Argive (Greek) youth. It is fun to consider that the pine planks were personified and the young men that ride them were, in effect, called trees.

5. **Colchīs** abl. pl., "from the Colchians."

6. **ausī sunt** A semi-deponent verb, translate "they dared."

7. Literally, "sweeping the sky blue flats with their fir palms." Welcome to poetic diction. How would we put it in plainer English?

Making Sense of It

Catullus sets the stage for his little epic, telling us that once Jason and other young men from Thessaly set out for Colchis where King Aeetes, the father of Medea, has possession of the golden fleece. According to legend this is the first time ships have taken to the sea. In the sections that follow we give you the first 15 lines of the epyllion, which is 408 lines long.

1   Quondam pīnūs prognātae (in) vertice Pēliacō

2   dīcuntur per undās liquidās Neptūnī nāsse

3   ad fluctūs et fīnēs Aeētēōs Phāsidos,

4   cum lectī iuvenēs, rōbora Argīvae pūbis,

5   (ā) Colchīs āvertere aurātam pellem optantēs

6   vada salsa citā puppī dēcurrere ausī sunt,

7   caerula aequora abiegnīs palmīs verrentēs.

Vocabulary

8. **dīvus, -a, -um** divine, as a noun, god or goddess
   retineō, -ēre, -uī, -tentum to hold fast, keep safe
   arx, arcis, f. a citadel, the fortified part of a city, usually located at its top

9. **volitō, -āre** to fly
   currus, -ūs, m. chariot
   flāmen, -inis, n. a gust of air

10. **pīneus, -a, -um** made of pine
    tegō, tegere, texī, tectum to weave
    īnflexus, -a, -um curved
    carīna, -ae, f. hull, by metonymy for the whole ship as **prora** was used above.
    coniungō, -ere, -iunxī, -iunctum to join together

11. **Amphitrītē, -ēs** f. (Greek endings) A sea goddess, wife of Neptune, and, by metonymy, "the sea"
    rudis, -e adj. here, "untrained," "unused to"
    cursus, -ūs, m. a running, a race. Here, the ship's path or journey
    imbuō, imbuere, imbuī, imbūtum to drench, to get wet, to dye; also (and especially here) to teach

12. **rostrum, -ī,** n. the prow of a ship; more particularly, its ramming beak.
    ventōsus, -a, -um windy
    prōscindō, -ere, -scidī, -scissum to tear into, to plow, cleave

13. **tortus, -a, -um** lit. "twisted," "turned," here, perhaps, "churned up."
    rēmigium, -ī, n. rowing
    spūma, -ae, f. foam, froth
    incānescō, -ere, incanuī to grow white

14. **ēmergō, -ere, -mersī, -mersum** to emerge, come out from
    ferus, -a, -um fierce, untamed
    candens, candentis (one-termination adj.) shining, glowing
    gurges, -itis, m. a whirlpool, often used as "the sea"
    vultus, -ūs, m. face

15. **Nēreis, -idis,** f. A sea goddess
    aequoreus, -a, -um see *aequor* l. 12
    admīror, -ārī, -ātus sum to admire, to marvel at

Notes

8. The **dīva** here is Athena, Jason's special protector who keeps the citadels of Thessaly safe for all the young men on the voyage.

9. **volitantem currum** the "flying chariot" is, again, the ship.

10. Athena, the goddess of crafts, is depicted as making the ship, fitting the pine planks to the hull.
    pīnea texta "The woven pine (things)".... i.e. the individual planks
    carīnae dative

11. As the first ship ever made, the Argo "taught" the sea (Amphitrite) a lesson with her journey (cursu). Note the built-in joke—**imbuō** means to get something wet and the ship, made wet by the sea, taught it something in turn. Catullus' friends would appreciate such a sophisticated word play.

13. A line that suffers from too many ablatives and not enough prepositions. The sea ("unda"), churned up by the rowing, grew white in its foam. Notice that what is plural (spūmīs) is better off as a singular in English and what is singular (unda) sounds better as a plural.

14. **ēmersēre.** An alternate, shortened form. What is the long form of this verb? You need to know this to read Catullus and poetry. If you have forgotten, see "Keep this Grammar in Mind," for Poem 8.
    ferī Nereids, sea goddesses, were beautiful creatures and *ferus* usually means "fierce." The sense might be "untamed" as yet by ships, "wild."

15. **mōnstrum** In its root meaning *mōnstrum* is something so unusual you will point it out (*mōnstrāre*). You might translate it here as "oddity."

Making Sense of It (CONTINUED)

The goddess Athena, who guards their citadels at home, helps them build the world's first ship and insures their safe journey. On the way sea goddesses stare up in wonder at what this new wonder might be.

8   Dīva (quae) rētinet (illīs iuvenibus) in summīs urbibus arcēs

9   ipsa fēcit volitantem currum levī flāmine,

10   pīnea texta īnflexae carīnae coniungēns;

11   illa prīma (navis) Amphitrītēn, rudem cursū, imbuit.

12   Quae (navis) simul ac rostrō ventōsum aequor prōscidit

13   et unda torta rēmigiō (ā) spūmīs incānuit,

14   ēmersēre ferī candentī ē gurgite vultūs,

15   aequoreae mōnstrum Nērēides admīrantēs.

WHAT CATULLUS ACTUALLY WROTE

As It Was

1   Pēliacō quondam prognātae vertice pīnūs

2   dīcuntur liquidās Neptūnī nāsse per undās

3   Phāsidos ad fluctūs et fīnēs Aeētēōs,

4   cum lectī iuvenēs, Argīvae rōbora pūbis,

5   aurātam optantēs Colchīs āvertere pellem

6   ausī sunt vada salsa citā dēcurrere puppī,

7   caerula verrentēs abiegnīs aequora palmīs.

8   Dīva quibus retinēns in summīs urbibus arcēs

9   ipsa levī fēcit volitantem flāmine currum,

10   pīnea coniungēns īnflexae texta carīnae;

11   illa rudem cursū prīma imbuit Amphitrītēn

12   quae simul ac rostrō ventōsum prōscidit aequor

13   tortaque rēmigiō spūmīs incānuit unda,

14   ēmersēre ferī candentī ē gurgite vultūs,

15   aequoreae mōnstrum Nērēides admīrantēs.

After Reading What Catullus Wrote

| Thinking about How the Author Writes | Metonymy and Elevated Language |

"And the pines sailed to Colchis," says Catullus, using part of a ship for the whole thing. Later the ship is referred to as "hull" or a "prow." Blades of oars are called "palms."

Elsewhere, just in these fifteen lines, he seems to have an aversion to plain speech, these same planks become the "woven piney things." The word **mare** is not to be found—instead we have "wave," "the flat expanse," "the salty deep," and "the whirlpool."

Such is the world of Alexandrian poetry, and, to a large extent, Roman poetry. Poets exult in the challenge of using a variety of ways to say the same thing. At first you might think it is alien to our mindset, but surely you know what the following phrases mean.

1. I want to go, but I don't have any **wheels** tonight.

2. The horse will not win today. It hasn't got **the legs** for this distance.

3. I'd pay, but I don't have **the cash/moolah/dough/scratch**.

4. Did you go shopping? You have new **threads** on.

5. Jeremiah! Get your sorry **bones** in this house this instant!

You can surely spot the uses of metonymy above and the alternates for common words are pretty obvious too. Can you think of some others that you use every day of your life?

Poetic Word Order

By now you have noticed that the word order used in this poem is extremely artificial. This is a common trait of Latin poetry and is not confined to the work of Catullus. At first it seems very difficult, but there are some tricks to learn that help us read it more readily.

First, though, let's investigate **why** poets did this. The first reason, of course, is that they are showing off, exhibiting their mastery of the language as they arrange words artistically within the confines of meter. But, of course, there is more to it than that. The main reason is that Latin allows words to be put next to each other to produce an effect that is totally impossible in English.

Synchesis

Consider the following sentence:

    A   **B**   **A**   **B**
Puer **puellam** *inelegāns* **candidam** amat.
The awkward boy loves the lovely girl.

In this sentence "boy" and "girl" and "lovely" and "clumsy" are put right next to each other to enhance the contrast. English cannot do this.

But if you try to create the same effect in English, you end up with **"The boy girl awkward lovely loves."** Just one more way Latin is superior to English!

Chiasmus

Consider this English sentence:

"Many people wish their friends well, but only a few also wish their enemies well."

You could say it this way in Latin, using a form of synchesis:

A   B   A   B
Multī amīcīs, sed paucī inimīcīs bene volunt.

Or you could rearrange it for effect:

A   B   B   A
Multī amīcīs, sed inimīcīs paucī bene volunt.

This **ABBA word order** is called **chiasmus**, after the Greek letter "chi," which resembles an X in English. The following diagram explains the derivation

English is far too dependent on word order to allow such things. But Latin poetry will often put words together in a line not just for "eye appeal" but also to enhance the meaning of the words as they appear next to each other in the line. This, by the way, is exactly why we read this poetry in the original Latin and not in English. In English you can get a sense of **what was said** but never a true sense of **how it was said.**

Hyperbaton

Finally, in addition to **chiasmus** and **synchesis** there is something called **hyperbaton**, which is Greek for "stepping over" and just means that the word order is violently disordered and related words are widely separated from one another.

Now It's Your Turn	TYPES OF WORD ORDER

Let's take another look at what you just read.

            A   B   A   B
1. Pēliacō quondam prognātae vertice pīnūs   synchesis

                    A   A
2. dīcuntur liquidās Neptūnī nāsse per undās   hyperbaton

3. Phāsidos ad fluctūs et fīnēs Aeētēōs,

                    A   A
4. cum lectī iuvenēs, Argīvae rōbora pūbis.   "sandwich"/bracketed

    A   A
5. Aurātam optantēs Colchīs āvertere pellem   hyperbaton

                 B   **B**

6. ausī sunt vada salsa citā dēcurrere puppī,   "sandwich"/bracketed

          A   **B**   **A**   **B**

7. caerula verrentēs abiegnīs aequora palmīs.   synchesis

Now, please mark and identify the word orders used in the sentences below.

8. Dīva quibus retinēns in summīs urbibus arcēs

9. ipsa levī fēcit volitantem flāmine currum,

10. pīnea coniungēns īnflexae texta carīnae;

11. illa rudem cursū prīma imbuit Amphitrītēn

12. quae simul ac rostrō ventōsum prōscidit aequor

13. tortaque rēmigiō spūmīs incānuit unda,

14. ēmersēre ferī candentī ē gurgite vultūs,

15. aequoreae mōnstrum Nērēides admīrantēs.

Final Thought and Hints

It should be clear by now that these are extremely common types of word order found in any poetry that strives to be formal and lofty in tone. You will see a great deal of this in Vergil, for example.

    Fortunately, there are ways to spot these types of word order early on and to adapt to their usage more quickly.

- **Mismatched Adjective and Noun Pairs**

When you have an adjective right next to a noun that it obviously cannot modify, be alert. When this occurs, especially at the beginning of a line, look for **chiasmus, synchesis,** or **hyperbaton.** Consider the following examples where we have highlighted the mismatched pairs.

    illa **rudem cursū** prīma imbuit Amphitrītēn
    dīcuntur **liquidās Neptūnī** nāsse per undās
    aequoreae mōnstrum Nērēides admīrantes.

- **Stranded Adjectives**

When you have an adjective on its own, early in the sentence and with no noun in sight, as in these examples, it is also a sign of poetic word order.

    ipsa **levī** fēcit volitantem **flāmine** currum,
    pīnea coniungēns īnflexae **texta** carīnae

Answers to Exercise A (p. 112)

1. Hephaestus/Vulcan
2. Hera/Juno
3. Prometheus
4. Davy Crockett
5. Paul Bunyan
6. George Washington
7. Pinocchio
8. Superman
9. Moses
10. John F. Kennedy
11. Batman/Bruce Wayne
12. Sherlock Holmes
13. Elvis Presley

CATULLUS 65.1-14

WRITER'S BLOCK I

BEFORE YOU READ WHAT CATULLUS WROTE

Introduction

This is a complex poem with many beautiful images and emotions. Catullus begins by apologizing to his friend Hortalus that he has not been more productively engaged with the Muses, but he has been so sad at the death of his brother, who died at Troy. Then he interrupts his letter to Hortalus to address his brother and express his undying love, alluding to the story of Philomela and Procne.

Procne (called Daulias in a typically learned Catullan allusion) killed her child to punish her husband for raping her sister. In the myth, Procne, her sister Philomela, and her husband Tereus are all turned into birds that sing mournful songs. Catullus compares his lament for his dead brother to the sad sound of Procne's song mourning the fate of her son.

Meter: Elegiac

Keep This Vocabulary in Mind

The syntax of this poem is very complex: the whole 24-line piece can be read as a single sentence. Fortunately the important part of this poem is the succession of images and emotions, not the syntax that holds them together.

Knowledge of the following proper nouns/adjectives will help you follow the flow of Catullus' narrative:

Hortalus:	Hortalus, the addressee of this poem, is a famous orator and friend of Catullus.
Musae:	The Muses, the nine virgin goddesses thought to inspire artistic creation, also called the learned virgins, *virginēs doctae*.
Lēthaeus:	Related to Lethe, the river of forgetfulness in the Underworld.
Trōius:	Trojan. Troy, traditionally a scene of heroic accomplishment, is for Catullus a scene of personal loss since his brother died there.
Rhoetēus:	The adjective Rhoetean refers to Rhoeteum, a town on the promontory near Troy. Catullus' brother was buried there. This type of specific geographical reference, rather than merely the general "Trojan" is typical of the Neoteric poets.
Daulias:	Daulian. Daulis is the city where Procne was turned to a swallow, so Catullus calls her "the Daulian."
Itylus:	Usually called Itys, Itylus is the son of Tereus and Procne. Procne, enraged at her husband for raping her sister, killed Itylus, cooked him and fed him to Tereus.

HELPING YOU READ WHAT CATULLUS WROTE

For this poem we give you font assistance but not rewrites.

Vocabulary

1. **etsī** conj. even if
   assiduus, -a, -um constant, unceasing
   cōnficiō, -ere, -fēcī, -fectum to finish, wear out
   cūra, -ae, f. care
   dolor, -ōris, m. grief, sadness

2. **sēvocō, -āre** to call apart, call away
   doctus, -a, -um learned
   Hortalus, -ī, m. Hortalus, an orator and poet in Catullus' circle of friends
   virgō, -inis, f. virgin

3. **Mūsae, -ārum,** f. pl. the Muses
   exprōmō, -ere to bring forth, display
   fētus, -ūs, m. offspring, fruit

4. **fluctuō, -āre** to undulate, be restless

5. **nūper** adv. recently
   Lēthaeus, -a, -um Lethean, of Lethe, a river of the Underworld
   gurges, -itis, m. stream, water

6. **pallidulus, -a, -um** pale little
   mānō, -āre to flow
   alluō, -ere, alluī to wash against
   pēs, pedis, m. foot

7. **Trōius, -a, -um** Trojan
   Rhoetēus, -a, -um Rhoetean, of Rhoeteum, a town on the Trojan promontory
   subter prep. + abl. beneath
   lītus, lītoris, n. shore
   tellūs, tellūris, f. earth

8. **ēripiō, -ere, ēripuī, ēreptum** to snatch away
   obterō, -ere to crush

Notes

1. **etsī** This conjunction sets up a complex syntactical structure. We do not even see the main clause of this sentence until *sed tamen* in line 15. Don't worry about it. The only difficulty to translating the opening of this poem is the word order. Try this: *Etsī cūra sēvocat mē cōnfectum assiduō dolōre ā doctīs virginibus, Hortale, . . .*

2. **doctīs . . . virginibus** See *Mūsae* under "Keep This Vocabulary in Mind," just above.

3. **potis . . . est = potest.**

4. **mēns animī** "(my) mind," the subject of *potis est.* **ipsa** refers to *mēns animī,* "it itself."

5. **namque = nam.** Try translating in this order: *nam nūper mānāns unda (in) Lēthaeō gurgite alluit pallidulum pedem meī frātris, . . .* Catullus cannot say anything so prosaic as "my brother died." The next couplet tells where he is buried.

7. Word order is again the trouble. Try: *quem, ēreptum ex nostrīs oculīs, Trōia tellūs obterit subter Rhoetēō lītore.*

9. Line 9 is missing from the manuscripts. By line 10, Catullus has interrupted his story to address his brother.

Making Sense of It

1   Etsī mē **assiduō** confectum cūra **dolōre**

2   sēvocat ā **doctīs**, Hortale, **virginibus**,

3   nec potis est **dulcīs** Mūsārum exprōmere **fētūs**

4   mēns animī, **tantīs** fluctuat ipsa **malīs** —

5   namque **meī** nūper Lēthaeō gurgite **frātris**

6   **pallidulum** mānāns alluit unda **pedem**,

7   **Trōia Rhoetēō** quem subter **lītore tellūs**

8   ēreptum **nostrīs** obterit ex **oculīs**.

9   **********************

Vocabulary

10. **numquam** adv. never
    amābilis, -e lovely, beloved

11. **aspiciō, -ere** to look upon
    posthāc adv. hereafter, in the future
    certē adv. certainly

12. **maestus, -a, -um** sad
    carmen, -minis, n. song, poem
    mors, mortis, f. death
    canō, -ere to sing

13. **quālis, -e** of what sort?
    dēnsus, -a, -um thick, dense
    rāmus, -ī, m. branch
    concinō, -ere to sing
    umbra, -ae, f. shade, shadow

14. **Daulias, -adis,** f. woman of Daulis: Procne
    absūmō, -ere, absumpsī, absumptum to take
       away
    fātum, -ī, n. death
    gemō, -ere to groan, lament

Notes

10. **ego tē** In Latin, the pronouns are usually
    bunched at the beginning of the sentence.
    Bring the verb *aspiciam* forward. Note that
    aspiciam, amābō, and *canam* are all in the same
    tense.
    vītā ablative of comparison with *amābilior.*

12. **tuā . . . morte** ablative of cause. Catullus' songs
    will be sad "because of your death."

13. **quālia . . . concinit . . . Daulias** "like the ones
    Procne sings."

14. **fāta** a poetic plural. Translate as though
    singular.

Making Sense of It (Continued)

10   Numquam ego tē, vītā frāter amābilior,

11   aspiciam posthāc? At certē semper amābō,

12   semper **maesta** *tuā* **carmina** *morte* canam,

13   qualia sub **dēnsīs** rāmōrum concinit **umbrīs**

14   Daulias *absumptī* fāta gemēns *Itylī*.

WHAT CATULLUS ACTUALLY WROTE

As It Was

1   Etsī mē assiduō confectum cūra dolōre

2   sēvocat ā doctīs, Hortale, virginibus,

3   nec potis est dulcīs Mūsārum exprōmere fētūs

4   mēns animī, tantīs fluctuat ipsa malīs —

5   namque meī nūper Lēthaeō gurgite frātris

6   pallidulum mānāns alluit unda pedem,

7   Trōia Rhoetēō quem subter lītore tellūs

8   ēreptum nostrīs obterit ex oculīs.

9   ********************

10   Numquam ego tē, vītā frāter amābilior,

11   aspiciam posthāc? At certē semper amābō,

12   semper maesta tuā carmina morte canam,

13   qualia sub dēnsīs rāmōrum concinit umbrīs

14   Daulias absumptī fāta gemēns Itylī.

AFTER READING WHAT CATULLUS WROTE

Thinking about What You Read

1. What does Catullus mean that care "calls [him] away from the learned virgins"?
2. Lines 1–4 are a complicated, poetic way of saying that sadness makes it impossible for Catullus to do what?
3. Why does Catullus call his brother's foot *pallidulum* (line 6)?
4. Why are Procne's songs an appropriate comparison for Catullus' songs?
5. What is odd about the comparison?

CATULLUS 65.15–24

WRITER'S BLOCK II

BEFORE YOU READ WHAT CATULLUS WROTE

Introduction

Even in the midst of sadness brought on by the death of his brother, Catullus was able to translate the lines of Callimachus that Hortalus had asked for and he is attaching them to this poem. In typical Neoteric style, Catullus does not call Callimachus by his name. Instead, because Callimachus was from Cyrene, he refers to him as Battiades, son of Battus, the ancient king of Cyrene, of whom we first heard in Poem 7. The next allusion is not to geography or literary history, but to Catullus' own poetry. He wants Hortalus to know that the promised translation has not been forgotten, and he uses the same image of words lost in the breeze that he uses in Poem 64 to describe Theseus' broken promises to Ariadne.

The poem ends with a beautiful and complex image of innocent forgetfulness. A maiden has received an apple as a secret gift from her fiancé and sits with it hidden beneath her tunic. She jumps up at the arrival of her mother and she is embarrassed when the apple rolls to the floor. Catullus assures Hortalus that his request has not slipped from his mind like this apple.

HELPING YOU READ WHAT CATULLUS WROTE

Vocabulary

15. maeror, -ōris, m. mourning

16. exprimō, -ere, expressī, expressum to translate
carmen, -minis, n. song, poem
Battiadēs, -ae, m. son of Battus; Callimachus

17. vagus, -a, -um wandering
nēquīquam adv. in vain
crēdō, -ere, crēdidī, crēditum entrust
ventus, -ī, m. wind

18. effluō, -ere, effluxī to flow out
forte by chance

19. spōnsus, -ī, m. fiancé
furtīvus, -a, -um secret
mūnus, mūneris, n. service, gift
mālum, -ī, n. apple

20. prōcurrō, -ere to run forth, rush out
castus, -a, -um chaste
gremium, -ī, n. lap

21. oblīviscor, -ī, oblītus sum to forget
vestis, -is, f. garment
locō, -āre, -āvī, -ātum to place

22. adventus, -ūs, m. arrival
prōsiliō, -īre to leap up
excutiō, -ere to shake out

23. prōnus, -a, -um downward
praeceps, -cipitis headlong
dēcursus, -ūs, m. course

24. mānō, -āre to flow
tristis, -e sad
cōnscius, -a, -um knowing
rubor, -ōris, m. blush

Notes

15. sed tamen answers the *etsī* from line 1: "Even though I have been distracted from my engagement with the Muses, I am sending you these translations."

15–16. Try reading it in this order: *Hortale, mittō tibī haec expressa carmina Battiadae*

16. haec expressa . . . carmina refers to the translations he is sending along with this poem. They are translations of the Greek poet Callimachus, a favorite of the Neoterics.

17. What kind of clause is **nē . . . forte putēs**? If you need a review see "Thinking about How the Author Writes," for Poem 5, above.
dicta = *verba*, "things that were said." It is the subject of *effluxisse* in the indirect statement, and is modified by the adjective phrase *nēquīquam crēdita vagīs ventīs*

19. ut "as," introducing a complicated simile.
spōnsī furtīvō mūnere "as a secret gift of her fiancé." Like Catullus with his translation, the girl is not yet ready for the world to see this gift.

21. quod The antecedent of this relative pronoun is *mālum.*
miserae oblītae "of the poor forgetful girl"

22. prōsilit The subject is the young girl, leaping up in surprise as her mother comes into the room.

23. illud refers to the apple; **huic** in line 24 refers to the girl. The apple charges thoughtlessly downward, while a knowing blush comes over the girl.

24. huic This is one of the datives we discussed above and is probably best translated as a genitive, "her."
tristī We have used fonts to show that *tristī* modifies *ore,* but it is worth considering that it might also be dative, modifying *huic.* Either way, it is clear that the girl is sad, a rather odd adjective to describe her. It connects her back to Catullus, sad at his brother's death.

Making Sense of It

15 Sed tamen in tantīs maerōribus, Hortale, mittō

16   haec expressa tibī carmina Battiadae

17 (nē tua **dicta** vagīs nēquīquam **crēdita** ventīs

18   effluxisse meō forte putēs animō),

19 ut *missum* spōnsī **furtīvō mūnere** *mālum*

20   prōcurrit castō virginis ē gremiō,

21 **quod** miserae oblītae mollī sub veste **locātum**,

22   dum adventū mātris prōsilit, excutitur,

23 atque illud *prōnō* praeceps agitur *dēcursū*,

24   huic mānat **tristī cōnscius ōre rubor**.

WHAT CATULLUS ACTUALLY WROTE

As It Was

15   Sed tamen in tantīs maerōribus, Hortale, mittō

16   haec expressa tibī carmina Battiadae

17   (nē tua dicta vagīs nēquīquam crēdita ventīs

18   effluxisse meō forte putēs animō),

19   ut missum spōnsī furtīvō mūnere mālum

20   prōcurrit castō virginis ē gremiō,

21   quod miserae oblītae mollī sub veste locātum,

22   dum adventū mātris prōsilit, excutitur,

23   atque illud prōnō praeceps agitur dēcursū,

24   huic mānat tristī cōnscius ōre rubor.

AFTER READING WHAT CATULLUS WROTE

Thinking about What You Read

1.   What happens to the girl and how does she react?

2.   To what does Catullus compare this?

3.   Why do you think Catullus ends the poem with so complicated an image?

APPENDIX A

GRAMMATICAL APPENDIX

SECTION 1: DECLENSIONS OF NOUNS

Nouns are the names of persons, places, or things. In Latin, nouns, pronouns, and adjectives are inflected to show their grammatical relations to the other words in the sentence. These inflectional endings are usually equivalent to prepositional phrases in English.

The names of the cases and their functions are as follows:

LATIN CASE	USE IN THE SENTENCE	ENGLISH CASE	EXAMPLE
Nominative	Subject or subj. complement.	Nominative.	puer (*the* or *a boy*)
Genitive	Shows possession and other relationships.	Possessive or the objective, with "of."	puerī (*of the boy*, or *of a boy or boy's*)
Dative	Indirect object and other relationships.	Objective, often with "to" or "for."	puerō (*to* or *for the boy*)
Accusative	Direct object.	Objective.	puerum (*boy,* or *the boy*)
Ablative	Occurs in adverbial phrases, usually with a preposition.	Objective, as object of many prepositions.	puerō (*by the boy, from, with, on, at,* etc.)

There are two additional cases which occur infrequently, and are not usually given with the decensions:

Vocative	Case of address. (The Latin inflectional ending is the same as in the nominative with exceptions noted, p. 136.)	Nominative of address.	puer! (*Boy!*)
Locative	Case of "place at which," with cities, towns, small islands, and **domus** (*home*), **rūs** (*country*), and **humus** (*the ground*) only.	Objective, with "at."	Rōmae (*at Rome*)

INFLECTION IN GENERAL

The inflectional ending of a word shows its *number, gender,* and *case.* The general concepts of number and case are similar to their counterparts in English (singular-plural, case structure outlined above). However, *gender* in Latin is often *grammatical* only, and unrelated to *natural* gender. Although there are the same three genders (masculine, feminine, neuter) in Latin as in English, it is not uncommon for a word like nauta *(sailor),* which is naturally male, to appear in a feminine declension (1st declension). Inflected words are composed of two parts: the *base* and the inflected portion. The *base* is that part of the word which remains unchanged, and the base of any noun may be determined by removing the ending of the *genitive singular* form. The base of **terra** is **terr-**; the base of **ager** is **agr-**, and so on.

FIRST AND SECOND DECLENSION NOUNS

The gender of most 1st declension nouns is feminine. That of most 2nd declension nouns is neuter (ending in **-um**) or masculine (ending in **-us** or **-er**).

1st Declension — Fem.

	Sing.	Plur.
Nom.	terra (*land*)	-ae
Gen.	terrae	-ārum
Dat.	terrae	-īs
Acc.	terram	-ās
Abl.	terrā	-īs

	2nd Declension — Masc.		2nd Declension — Neut.		2nd Declension Masc. Ending in -er			
	Sing.	Plur.	Sing.	Plur.	Sing.	Plur.	Sing.	Plur.
Nom.	animus (*mind*)	-ī	caelum (*sky*)	-a	magister (*teacher*)	-ī	puer (*boy*)	-ī
Gen.	animī	-ōrum	caelī	-ōrum	magistrī	-ōrum	puerī	-ōrum
Dat.	animō	-īs	caelō	-īs	magistrō	-īs	puerō	-īs
Acc.	animum	-ōs	caelum	-a	magistrum	-ōs	puerum	-ōs
Abl.	animō	-īs	caelō	-īs	magistrō	-īs	puerō	-īs

THIRD DECLENSION NOUNS

The trademark of the 3rd declension is the ending **-is** in the genitive singular. It is added to the base. All genders are represented in the 3rd declension.[1]

	Sing.	Plur.		Sing.	Plur.		Sing.	Plur.		Sing	Plur.
Nom.	lux (light)	lūcēs		parens (parent)	parentēs		nāvis (ship)	-ēs		nox (night)	noctēs
Gen.	lūcis	-um		parentis	-um		nāvis	-ium		noctis	-ium
Dat.	lūcī	-ibus		parentī	-ibus		nāvī	-ibus		noctī	-ibus
Acc.	lūcem	-ēs		parentem	-ēs		nāvem	-ēs (-īs)		noctem	-ēs (-īs)
Abl.	lūce	-ibus		parente	-ibus		nāve	-ibus		nocte	-ibus

	Sing.	Plur.		Sing.	Plur.		Sing.	Plur.
Nom.	mare (sea)	-ia		genus (type)	genera		flūmen (river)	flūmina
Gen.	maris	-ium		generis	-um		flūminis	-um
Dat.	marī	-ibus		generī	-ibus		flūminī	-ibus
Acc.	mare	-ia		genus	-a		flūmen	-a
Abl.	marī	-ibus		genere	-ibus		flūmine	-ibus

[1] Nouns ending in **-is** or **-es** that have the same number of syllables in the genitive and the nominative take **-ium** in the genitive plural and, sometimes, **-īs** in the accusative plural.

Nouns whose bases end in double consonants take **-ium** in the genitive plural and, sometimes, **-īs** in the accusative plural.

Neuter nouns ending in **-e, -al,** or **-ar** take **-ī** in the ablative singular, **-ia** in the nominative and accusative plural, and **-ium** in the genitive plural.

IRREGULAR NOUNS OF THE THIRD DECLENSION

A. **Vīs** (*force in sing.,* strength *in plur.*), fem., is declined **vīs, vis, vī, vim, vī,** (plur.) **vīrēs, vīrium, vīribus, vīrēs (-īs), vīribus.**

B. **Puppis, puppis** (*stern, ship*), fem., and **turris, turris** (*tower*), fem., usually have **-im** in the accusative singular, and **-ī** in the ablative singular.

C. The ablative in **-ī** is occasionally used with i-stem nouns like **classis, classis** (*fleet*).

D. **Senex, senis** (*old man*), masc., has **senum** in the genitive plural.

E. The declension of **Iuppiter** (*Jupiter*): **Iuppiter, Iovis, Iovī, Iovem, Iove.**

F. **Hērōs, hērōis, hērōī, hērōa, hērōe** is a Greek masc. noun meaning *hero.*

G. **Īlias, Īliados** (*Iliad*), fem., is declined like **hērōs.**

FOURTH DECLENSION NOUNS

Most 4th declension nouns are masculine and are formed from the 4th principal part of the verb.

	Masc.		Fem.		Neut.	
	Sing.	Plur.	Sing.	Plur.	Sing.	Plur.
Nom.	portus (port)	-ūs	domus (house)	-ūs	cornū (horn)	-ua
Gen.	portūs	-uum	domūs (-ī)	-uum (-ōrum)	cornūs	-uum
Dat.	portuī (-ū)	-ibus	domuī (-ō)	-ibus	cornū	-ibus
Acc.	portum	-ūs	domum	-ōs (-ūs)	cornū	-ua
Abl.	portū	-ibus	domū (-ō)	-ibus	cornū	-ibus

FIFTH DECLENSION NOUNS

Very few nouns in the 5th declension are declined throughout. Most fifth declension nouns are rarely found in the genitive, dative, and ablative plural.

All 5th declension nouns are feminine except **merīdiēs,** which is masculine, and **diēs,** which is either masculine or feminine in the singular but always masculine in the plural.

	Sing.	Plur.		Sing.	Plur.
Nom.	diēs (day)	diēs		rēs (matter)	rēs
Gen.	diēī	diērum		reī	rērum
Dat.	diēī	diēbus		reī	rēbus
Acc.	diem	diēs		rem	rēs
Abl.	diē	diēbus		rē	rēbus

SECTION 2: SYNTAX OF CASES

NOMINATIVE CASE

1. The subject of a finite verb is nominative. **Catullus** obdūrat. *Catullus is holding strong.*
2. Predicate Nominative (Subject Complement). After the verb *to be* or any form thereof the subject complement replaces an object of the verb. It is in the same case as the subject. Suffēnus est **homō** venustus. *Suffēnus is a charming person.*

GENITIVE CASE

1. Possession. **Lesbiae** passer *Lesbia's sparrow.* BUT: rēgīna **mea** *my queen* (Possessive adjective)
2. Quality (When a noun is modified). **Tantae mōlis** erat condere. *Founding was of so great an effort.*
3. Subjective. **caelī** furor *the fury of the sky*
4. Objective. meus amor **Lesbiae** *my love of Lesbia* (= I love Lesbia)
5. Partitive: nūlla mīca **sālis** *no grain of salt* Note: The following adjectives modify their noun directly and are not followed by the genitive:

    omnis — *all of*   summus — *top of*
    tōtus — *whole of*   medius — *middle of*

    Cardinal numerals and quīdam take ex or dē plus the ablative case rather than the partitive genitive. (See "Ablative With Cardinal Numbers" below.)
6. With verbs of reminding, remembering and forgetting. **huius** meminisse *to remember this (day)* Note: To remember or forget a *thing* is rendered by meminī plus the accusative case: **haec** meminisse *to remember these things*
7. Verbs of accusing or condemning take the genitive. damnātī **mortis** *convicted of the death*
8. With miseret, paenitet, piget, pudet, and taedet, the genitive is used as the cause of the feeling. Lesbia, **meī** miserēre. *Lesbia, have mercy on me!*
9. Genitive of Price. **ūnius assis** *worth a single penny*
10. Genitive of Respect or Specification. Plēnus sacculus est **arāneārum**. *My purse is filled with cobwebs.*

DATIVE CASE

1. Indirect object. **Cui** dōnō? *To whom am I giving?*
2. Indirect object with intransitive and passive verbs. Quae **tibī** manet vīta? *What life remains for you?*
3. Indirect object with compound verbs. Some verbs are compounded with ad, ante, con, in, ob, post, prae, prō, sub, super in such a way as to change their meanings and call for a dative object. Catullus **Caesarī** nōn adsentitur. *Catullus does not agree with Caesar.*
4. Dative of Possession (with the verb *to be*, either expressed or understood). **Lesbiae** multī amantēs sunt. *Lesbia has many lovers.* Note how the dative of possession is usually translated into English as the subject of the verb *to have.*
5. Dative of Agent is used with some of the perfect passive constructions (and with gerundives) to show the "doer" of the action. **Nōbīs** . . . nox est perpetua ūna dormienda. *There is one perpetual night to be slept by us.*
6. Dative of Purpose. Ōtium **curae** est. *Leisure is a source of concern.*
7. Dative of Reference. The person or thing affected in the sentence: Ōtium **tibi** molestum est. *Leisure is troublesome for you.* Note: When the datives of purpose and reference are used together (as in **Catullō** Fabullus **amicō** est. *Fabullus is like a friend to Catullus.*), they are called the double dative.
8. Dative of Separation. Occasionally, after compounds with ab, dē, ex, ad, the dative occurs instead of the usual ablative. Tam bellum **mihi** passerem abstulistis. *You have taken away so beautiful a sparrow from me.*
9. The dative occurs with adjectives of *fitness* (aptus), *nearness* (proximus), *likeness* (similis), *friendliness* (amīcus), and their opposites. par **deō** *equal to a god*

ACCUSATIVE CASE

1. Direct object of a transitive verb. superāre **deōs** *to surpass the gods*
2. Subject of the infinitive. In indirect statements and after iubeō (*order*), patior (*allow*), and sinō (*permit*), the subject of the infinitive goes into the accusative case. Tū solēbās // **meās** esse aliquid putāre **nūgās**. *You were accustomed to think that my trifles were actually something.*
3. Predicate accusative or object complement where a second accusative is used after verbs like appellō (*name*), dēligō (*choose*), faciō (*make*). Rogābis deōs ut tē faciant, Fabulle, **tōtum nāsum**. *Fabullus, you will ask the gods to make you all nose!*
4. Accusative of Extent (how long in time or space). Also called accusative of duration of time. trīgintā **annōs** *for thirty years*
5. Accusative of Place to Which. Catullus **ad forum** venit. *Catullus is coming to the forum.*
6. Accusative with middle/passive verbs. Catullus **sententiam** rogātus est. *Catullus was asked his opinion.*
7. Accusative of Exclamation. **Miserum**! *The wretch!*
8. Object of certain prepositions. These prepositions take an accusative object: ad, ante, circum, contrā, inter, intrā, ob, per, post, prope, propter, super, trāns, ultrā. **multa** per **aequora** vectus *borne over many oceans* See prepositions below.
9. Accusative supine after a verb of motion to express purpose. Veniam **nuntiātum**. *I will go to make the announcement.*

ABLATIVE CASE

1. Object of certain prepositions (all those not listed as governing the accusative case). The more common ones are ā/ab, cum, dē, ē/ex, in, prae, prō, sine, sub. sub **dēnsīs umbrīs** *under dense shadows* See prepositions below.

2. Personal agent, expressed with a passive verb and a person, with ā /ab. ā **Catullō** *by Catullus*

3. Separation. Sēvocat mē ā **doctīs virginibus.** *He calls me away from the learned virgins (Muses).*

4. Place from which. Catullus ā **forō** venit. *Catullus is coming from the Forum.*

5. Ablative with Cardinal Numbers. Duo dē **numerō.** *Two of the number.*

6. Ablative of Cause. maesta **tuā** carmina **morte** *songs sad because of your death*

7. Ablative of Means. **pūmice** expolītum *polished with pumice*

8. Ablatives with Special Verbs. With the deponent verbs ūtor (*use*), fruor (*enjoy*), fungor (*accomplish*), potior (*gain*), and vēscor (*feed on*), the ablative is usually used. **Hīs vocibus** ūsa est. *She used these words.*

9. Ablative with opus and ūsus (meaning *need*). Mille **bāsiīs** opus est. *There is need of a thousand kisses.*

10. Ablative of Accordance. **spontē suā** *of his own accord*

11. Ablative of Place Where (usually, but not always, with a preposition like *in*). **Tōtō lectō** versarer. *I was tossing all over the bed.* If the preposition is omitted with names of towns, *domus, rūs,* and *humus,* the locative case is used (see below).

12. Ablative of Comparison. When quam (*than*) is omitted in comparisons, the ablative is used. plūs **ūnō saeclō** *more than a single age*

13. Degree of Difference: After comparatives, this ablative shows the extent or degree to which the objects differ. **Multō** es vīlior. *You are much cheaper.*

14. Ablative of Manner, telling "how," may omit the usual cum if the noun is modified. **modīs** pallida **mīrīs.** *pale in a marvelous manner* **prīscō** quae **mōre** parentum *in the ancient tradition of our parents*

15. Accompaniment. cum **moechīs suīs** *with her adulterers*

16. Ablative of Time When, without a preposition. **hesternō diē** *yesterday*

17. Ablative Absolute: This construction consists of a noun or pronoun in the ablative case plus a present active or perfect passive participle, or two nouns in the ablative case, or a noun and an adjective, with the participle understood. The construction is usually translated by a clause referring to time (*when*), cause (*since, because*), concession (*although*), condition (*if*). In any given instance any of the above translations may be appropriate, depending upon the sense of the rest of the context. **virō praesente** *with her husband present*

18. Quality or Description: **pulchrā orīgine** Caesar *Caesar of beautiful origin*

VOCATIVE CASE

The vocative case is used for direct address. Its forms are exactly like those of the nominative case, except for 2nd declension nouns ending in -us or -ius. **Cornēlī, tibi** *Cornelius, (I am giving it) to you* **mī Fabulle** *my Fabullus!*

LOCATIVE CASE

The locative case is used only to indicate "place where" or "place at which" with names of towns or cities, humus (*soil*), domus (*home*), and rūs (*the country*). In all other cases the ablative of "place where" with the preposition *in* is used. The locative endings are:

	Sing.	*Plur.*
1st Declension	-ae	-īs
2nd Declension	-ī	-īs
3rd Declension	-ī or -e	-ibus

Rōmae — *in Rome,* **domī** — *at home,* **rūrī** — *in the country*

PREPOSITIONS, PREFIXES

Most of the prepositions in Latin are used to govern the use of the accusative case. About one third of them govern the ablative, and a few govern both cases, depending upon the verb used in the sentence. Many prepositions are also commonly used as prefixes. Attached to the front of a word, they give it a different shade of meaning. Examples are below.

PREPOSITION	CASE	MEANING	COMPOUND	MEANING
ā, ab	Ablative	*away from*	**ab**dūcō	*lead away*
ad	Accusative	*to*	**ad**dūcō	*lead to, influence*
ante	Accusative	*before*	**ante**ferō	*bear before*
apud	Accusative	*at, among*		
circum	Accusative	*around, about*	**circum**ferō	*carry around*
contrā	Accusative	*against*		
cum, con, com	Ablative	*with*	**con**trahō	*draw together*
dē	Ablative	*down from*	**dē**scendō	*climb down*
ē, ex	Ablative	*out from*	**ex**pellō	*drive out*
in	Accusative	*into*	**in**iciō	*hurl into*
in	Ablative	*in (place where)*		
inter	Accusative	*between, among*	**inter**rumpō	*interrupt*
ob	Accusative	*on account of*	**oc**currō	*run to meet*
per	Accusative	*through*	**per**rumpō	*break through*
post	Accusative	*after*	**post**pōnō	*put after*
prae	Ablative	*in front of*	**prae**ficiō	*put in command*
praeter	Accusative	*along by, past*	**praeter**eō	*go past*
prō	Ablative	*in front of*	**prō**dūcō	*lead forth*
propter	Accusative	*on account of*		
re-, red-	Prefix only	*back*	**red**imō	*buy back*
sub	Accusative	*up from under*	**sub**eō	*approach*
sub	Ablative	*under*	**sub**trahō	*draw from under*
super	Accusative	*above*	**super**immineō	*tower over*
trāns	Accusative	*across*	**trāns**eō	*go across*
ultrā	Accusative	*beyond*		

SECTION 3: PRONOUNS

Pronouns, as the name implies, take the place of nouns. At times, they are used as adjectives, to modify nouns. Under those circumstances, they agree with the nouns in gender, number, and case.

PERSONAL PRONOUNS

		1st Person					2nd Person		
	Sing.		*Plur.*			*Sing.*		*Plur.*	
Nom.	ego	*I*	nōs	*we*	tū	*you*	vōs	*you*	
Gen.	meī	*of me*	nostrum, nostrī	*of us*	tuī	*of you*	vestrum, vestrī	*of you*	
Dat.	mihi	*to me*	nōbīs	*to us*	tibi	*to you*	vōbīs	*to you*	
Acc.	mē	*me*	nōs	*us*	tē	*you*	vōs	*you*	
Abl.	mē	*by, etc., me*	nōbīs	*by, etc., us*	tē	*by, etc., you*	vōbīs	*by, etc., you*	

3rd Person: A demonstrative pronoun is used as the pronoun of the 3rd person.

The Demonstrative Pronouns (or Adjectives)

There are five demonstratives used to point out special objects or persons.

      Hic (*this here*) refers to what is near the speaker in place, time, or thought. Sometimes the word may also mean *he, she,* or *it.*

      Ille (*that there*) refers to something remote from the speaker. It also means *that famous.*

      Is, ea, id are most commonly used for *he, she,* or *it.* They may also mean *this* or *that.*

      Iste (*that — nearby* or *that of yours*) is often used comtemptuously.

      Īdem means *the same.*

Masc.	*Fem.*	*Neut.*	*Masc.*	*Fem.*	*Neut.*	*Masc.*	*Fem.*	*Neut.*	*Masc.*	*F em.*	*Neut.*
hic	haec	hoc	ille	illa	illud	is	ea	id	iste	ista	istud
huius	huius	huius	illīus	illīus	illīus	ēius	ēius	ēius	istīus	istīus	istīus
huic	huic	huic	illī	illī	illī	eī	eī	eī	istī	istī	istī
hunc	hanc	hoc	illum	illam	illud	eum	eam	id	istum	istam	istud
hōc	hāc	hōc	illō	illā	illō	eō	eā	eō	istō	istā	istō
hī	hae	haec	illī	illae	illa	eī	eae	ea	istī	istae	ista
hōrum	hārum	hōrum	illōrum	illārum	illōrum	eōrum	eārum	eōrum	istōrum	istārum	istōrum
hīs	hīs	hīs	illīs	illīs	illīs	eīs	eīs	eīs	istīs	istīs	istīs
hōs	hās	haec	illōs	illās	illa	eōs	eās	ea	istōs	istās	ista
hīs	hīs	hīs	illīs	illīs	illīs	eīs	eīs	eīs	istīs	istīs	istīs

Masc.	*Fem.*	*Neut.*
īdem	eadem	idem
eiusdem	eiusdem	eiusdem
eīdem	eīdem	eīdem
eundem	eandem	idem
eōdem	eādem	eōdem
eīdem	eaedem	eadem
eōrundem	eārundem	eōrundem
eīsdem	eīsdem	eīsdem
eōsdem	eāsdem	eadem
eīsdem	eīsdem	eīsdem

Indefinite Pronouns

Quis, aliquis, and **quīdam** are the indefinite pronouns. **Quis** is usually used immediately after sī, nisi, nē, and num. Only the quis and quī of the indefinites may be declined: **quis** is declined like the interrogative below; **quī** is declined like the relative.

Interrogative Pronouns

The interrogative pronoun, as its name implies, introduces a question. **Quis** means *who,* and **quid** means *what.* Declension is like the relative, **quis** for **quī**, **quid** for **quod,** with the plural declined the same.

Possessive Pronouns (or Adjectives)

1st Person Sing.
meus, -a, -um *my, mine*
(Declined like bonus)

1st Person Plur.
noster, nostra, nostrum
(Declined like pulcher)

2nd Person Sing.
tuus, tua, tuum *your*

2nd Person Plur.
vester, vestra, vestrum

3rd Person Reflexive Possessive
suus, sua, suum *his, her, its, their*

Suus refers to the subject and agrees with the noun modified in gender, number, and case.

REFLEXIVE PRONOUNS

The reflexive pronoun of the third person has a single declension for singular and plural, and all three genders.

Nom.	(none)
Gen.	suī
Dat.	sibi
Acc.	sē
Abl.	sē

Note: The oblique cases of the 1st and 2nd person of the *personal* pronouns are used reflexively. Amō **mē.** (*I love myself.*)

THE INTENSIVE PRONOUN IPSE

Ipse is used to emphasize nouns and pronouns of any person and agrees with the pronoun contained in the verb. Aenēās **ipse** haec dīxit. *Aeneas himself said these things.*

Sing.			*Plur.*		
ipse	ipsa	ipsum	ipsī	ipsae	ipsa
ipsīus	ipsīus	ipsīus	ipsōrum	ipsārum	ipsōrum
ipsī	ipsī	ipsī	ipsīs	ipsīs	ipsīs
ipsum	ipsam	ipsum	ipsōs	ipsās	ipsa
ipsō	ipsā	ipsō	ipsīs	ipsīs	ipsīs

RELATIVE PRONOUNS

Quī, quae, quod (*who, which*) is the most commonly used of the relative pronouns (or adjectives).

	Sing.			*Plur.*	
Masc.	*Fem.*	*Neut.*	*Masc.*	*Fem.*	*Neut.*
quī	quae	quod	quī	quae	quae
cuius	cuius	cuius	quōrum	quārum	quōrum
cui	cui	cui	quibus	quibus	quibus
quem	quam	quod	quōs	quās	quae
quō	quā	quō	quibus	quibus	quibus

SECTION 4: ADJECTIVES AND ADVERBS

FIRST AND SECOND DECLENSION ADJECTIVES

Adjectives agree with their nouns in gender, number, and case. Those in the predicate after **sum** (*be*) agree with the subject, as in English. Most masculine adjectives are declined like **ager, puer,** or **dominus;** neuter adjectives like **caelum;** and feminine adjectives like **terra.**

	Masculine		Feminine		Neuter	
	Sing.	*Plur.*	*Sing.*	*Plur.*	*Sing.*	*Plur.*
Nom.	bonus	-ī	bona	-ae	bonum	-a
Gen.	bonī	-ōrum	bonae	-ārum	bonī	-ōrum
Dat.	bonō	-īs	bonae	-īs	bonō	-īs
Acc.	bonum	-ōs	bonam	-ās	bonum	-a
Abl.	bonō	-īs	bonā	-īs	bonō	-īs

THIRD DECLENSION ADJECTIVES

Third declension adjectives fall into four distinct categories: (1) *three-termination*, with separate endings for all three genders, like **ācer**; (2) *two-termination*, with the same endings for masculine and feminine, like **omnis**; (3) *one-termination*, with the nominative singular the same in all genders, like **potēns**; and (4) the *comparative* of all adjectives, like **longior**. The forms of **plūs** (5) are unique. Present participles are declined like **potēns**.

(1) ācer (keen)

	Masc. Sing.	Masc. Plur.	Fem. Sing.	Fem. Plur.	Neut. Sing.	Neut. Plur.
Nom.	ācer	ācrēs	ācris	ācrēs	ācre	ācria
Gen.	ācris	-ium	ācris	-ium	ācris	-ium
Dat.	ācrī	-ibus	ācrī	-ibus	ācrī	-ibus
Acc.	ācrem	-ēs (-īs)	ācrem	-ēs (-īs)	ācre	-ia
Abl.	ācrī	-ibus	ācrī	-ibus	ācrī	-ibus

(2) omnis (every, all)

	Masc. & Fem. Sing.	Masc. & Fem. Plur.	Neut. Sing.	Neut. Plur.
Nom.	omnis	-ēs	omne	-ia
Gen.	omnis	-ium	omnis	-ium
Dat.	omnī	-ibus	omnī	-ibus
Acc.	omnem	-ēs (-īs)	omne	-ia
Abl.	omnī	-ibus	omnī	-ibus

(3) potēns (powerful)

	Masc. & Fem. Sing.	Masc. & Fem. Plur.	Neut. Sing.	Neut. Plur.
Nom.	potēns	potentēs	potēns	potentia
Gen.	potentis	-ium	potentis	-ium
Dat.	potentī	-ibus	potentī	-ibus
Acc.	potentem	-ēs (-īs)	potēns	-ia
Abl.	potentī (-e)	-ibus	potentī (-e)	-ibus

(4) longior (longer)

	Masc. & Fem. Sing.	Masc. & Fem. Plur.	Neut. Sing.	Neut. Plur.
Nom.	longior	longiōrēs	longius	longiōra
Gen.	longiōris	-um	longiōris	-um
Dat.	longiōrī	-ibus	longiōrī	-ibus
Acc.	longiōrem	-ēs (-īs)	longius	-a
Abl.	longiōre	-ibus	longiōre	-ibus

(5) plūs (more)

	Masc. & Fem. Plur.	Neut. Sing.	Neut. Plur.
Nom.	plūrēs	plūs	plūra
Gen.	-ium	plūris	-ium
Dat.	-ibus	plūrī	-ibus
Acc.	-ēs (-īs)	plūs	-a
Abl.	-ibus	plūre	-ibus

THE NINE IRREGULAR ADJECTIVES

There are nine adjectives ("the naughty nine") which are regular in the plural and irregular in the singular. The plurals of these words are declined like **bonus**. With the exceptions noted, the *singulars* of these adjectives are declined like **tōtus**.

alius	*other, another* (neut. — aliud)	alter	*the other* (gen. — alterīus)
ūllus	*any*	nūllus	*no, none*
ūnus	*one, alone*	sōlus	*alone, only*
neuter	*neither* (gen. — neutrīus)	uter	*which of two* (gen. — utrīus)

tōtus (whole, all)

	Masc.	Fem.	Neut.
Nom.	tōtus	tōta	tōtum
Gen.	tōtīus	tōtīus	tōtīus
Dat.	tōtī	tōtī	tōtī
Acc.	tōtum	tōtam	tōtum
Abl.	tōtō	tōtā	tōtō

NUMERALS

Of the numerals, only **ūnus, duo, trēs,** the hundreds, and the plural of **mīlle** are declined.

	ŪNUS M.	ŪNUS F.	ŪNUS N.	DUO M.	DUO F.	DUO N.	TRĒS M. & F.	TRĒS N.	MĪLLE P. only
Nom.	ūnus	ūna	ūnum	duo	duae	duo	trēs	tria	mīlia
Gen.	ūnīus	ūnīus	ūnīus	duōrum	duārum	duōrum	trium	trium	mīlium
Dat.	ūnī	ūnī	ūnī	duōbus	duābus	duōbus	tribus	tribus	mīlibus
Acc.	ūnum	ūnam	ūnum	duōs	duās	duo	trēs (-īs)	tria	milia
Abl.	ūnō	ūnā	ūnō	duōbus	duābus	duōbus	tribus	tribus	mīlibus

There are four types of numerals: Cardinal Numerals (adjectives) one, two, etc.; Ordinal Numerals (adjectives) first, second, etc.; Distributives (adjectives) one by one, two by two, three each, etc.; Numerical Adverbs (once, twice, etc.).

	CARDINALS	ORDINALS	DISTRIBUTIVES	ADVERBS	NUMERALS
1	ūnus, -a, -um	prīmus, -a, -um	singulī, -ae, -a	semel	I
2	duo, duae, duo	secundus	bīnī	bis	II
3	trēs, tria	tertius	ternī (trinī)	ter	III
4	quattuor	quārtus	quaternī	quater	IV
5	quinque	quintus	quīnī	quinquiens	V
6	sex	sextus	sēnī	sexiens	VI
7	septem	septimus	septēnī	septiens	VII
8	octō	octāvus	octōnī	octiens	VIII
9	novem	nōnus	novēnī	noviens	IX
10	decem	decimus	dēnī	deciens	X
11	undecim	undecimus	undēnī	ndeciens	XI
12	duodecim	duodecimus	duodēnī	duodeciens	XII
13	tredecim	tertius decimus	ternī dēnī	terdeciens	XIII
14	quattuordecim	quārtus decimus	quaternī dēnī	quater deciens	XIV
15	quindecim	quintus decimus	quīnī dēnī	quīndeciens	XV
16	sēdecim	sextus decimus	sēnī dēnī	sēdeciens	XVI
17	septendecim	septimus decimus	septēnī dēnī	septiens deciens	XVII
18	duodēvīgintī	duodēvīcēsimus	duodēvīcēnī	duodēvīciens	XVIII
	(octōdecim)	(octāvus decimus)	(octōnī dēnī)	(octiens deciens)	
19	undēvīgintī	undēvīcēsimus	undēvīcēnī	undēvīciens	XIX
	(novendecim)	(nōnus decimus)	(novēnī dēnī)	(noviens deciens)	
20	vīgintī	vīcēsimus	vīcēnī	vīciens	XX
21	vīgintī ūnus	ūnus et vīcēsimus	vīcēnī singulī	vīciens semel	XXI
30	trīgintā	trīcēsimus	trīcēnī	trīciens	XXX
40	quadrāgintā	quadrāgēsimus	quadrāgēnī	quadrāgiens	XL
50	quinquāgintā	quinquāgēsimus	quinquāgēnī	quīnquāgiens	L
60	sexāgintā	sexāgēsimus	sexāgēnī	sexāgiens	LX
70	septuāgintā	septuāgēsimus	septuāgēnī	septuāgiens	LXX
80	octōgintā	octōgēsimus	octōgēnī	octōgiens	LXXX
90	nōnāgintā	nōnāgēsimus	nōnāgēnī	nōnāgiens	XC
100	centum	centēsimus	centēnī	centiens	C
101	centum ūnus	centēsimus prīmus	centēnī singulī	centiens semel	CI
200	ducentī, -ae, -a	duocentēsimus	ducēnī	ducentiens	CC
300	trecentī	trecentēsimus	trecēnī	trecentiens	CCC
400	quadringentī	quadringentēsimus	quadringēnī	quadringentiens	CCCC
500	quingentī	quingentēsimus	quingēnī	quingentiens	D
1000	mīlle	mīllēsimus	mīllenī	mīlliens	M
2000	duo mīlia	bis mīllēsimus	bīna mīlia	bis mīlliens	MM

COMPARISON OF ADJECTIVES

There are three degrees of comparison in Latin, just as there are in English: *positive, comparative,* and *superlative.* The *comparative* is formed by adding **-ior** for the masculine and feminine, and **-ius** for the neuter to the base of the *positive.* The *superlative* is formed by adding **-issimus, -a, -um** to the base. The *comparative* is declined like **longior** (see Section 4); the *positive* is declined like **bonus** for 1st and 2nd declension, like **omnis** for third declension adjectives (see also Section 4). The *superlative* is declined like **bonus.**

Note: Six adjectives ending in **-lis** (facilis, difficilis, similis, dissimilis, gracilis, humilis) add **-limus** instead of -issimus to the base to form the *superlative:* (facilis, facilior, facillimus)

Note: Adjectives ending in **-er** add **-rimus** instead of -issimus to form the *superlative.*

miser, -a, -um	miserior, miserius	miserrimus, -a, -um
ācer, ācris, ācre	ācrior, ācrius	ācerrimus, -a, -um

Note: Adjectives ending in **-ius** or **-eus** add **magis** to form the comparative and **maximē** to form the superlative: idōneus, magis idōneus, maximē idōneus.

REGULAR FORMS			IRREGULAR COMPARISONS		
POSITIVE	COMPARATIVE	SUPERLATIVE	POSITIVE	COMPARATIVE	SUPERLATIVE
longus, -a, -um	longior, longius	longissimus, -a, -um	bonus (*good*)	melior	optimus
fortis, forte	fortior, fortius	fortissimus, -a, -um	malus (*bad*)	peior	pessimus
			magnus (*large*)	maior	maximus
			multus (*much*)	plūs	plūrimus
			multī (*many*)	plūrēs	plūrimī
			parvus (*small*)	minor	minimus

FORMATION AND COMPARISON OF ADVERBS

Positive adverbs are formed regularly by adding **-ē** to the base of adjectives of the 1st and 2nd declensions (longē). Adjectives of the 3rd declension may be changed to adverbs by adding **-iter** to the base (fortiter). Those with a base of **-nt** simply add **-er** (prūdenter). Examples are below.

POSITIVE	COMPARATIVE	SUPERLATIVE
longē	longius	longissimē
fortiter	fortius	fortissimē
miserē	miserius	miserrimē
ācriter	ācrius	ācerrimē
facile	facilius	facillimē
bene	melius	optimē
male	pēius	pessimē
magnopere	magis	maximē
multum	plūs	plūrimum
parum	minus	minimē
diū	diūtius	diūtissimē

ADVERBS OF LOCATION

hīc (here)	hinc (from here)	hūc (to here)	hāc (by this way)	ultrō (beyond)
ibi (there)	inde (from there)	eō (to there)	eā (by that way)	usquam (anywhere)
illīc (there)	illinc (from there)	illūc (to there)	illā (by that way)	nusquam (nowhere)
istīc (there)	istinc (from there)	istūc (to there)	istā (by that way)	intrō (inwardly, from the outside in)
ubi (where)	unde (from where)	quō (to where)	quā (by what way)	extrō (outwardly, from the inside out)

ADVERBS OF TIME

cum (when)	hodiē (today)	iamdudum (now for a long time)	numquam (never)	quandō (when?)	umquam (ever)
deinde (next)	iam (already)	mox (soon)	prīdem (long ago)	saepe (often)	ut (when)
dum (while)	iam diū (long ago)	nōndum (not yet)	prīmum (first)	semper (always)	

INTERROGATIVE ADVERBS

-ne, an enclitic, expects a yes or no answer
> Sīcine mē līquistī? (*Did you leave me thus?*)

Num expects the answer *"no."*
> **Num** tē leaena prōcreāvit? (*A lion didn't give birth to you, did it?*)

Nōnne expects the answer *"yes."*
> **Nōnne** mē amās? (*Don't you love me?*)

An, -ne, anne, utrum, num, introducing indirect questions, all mean *"whether."*
> **An** ut perveniās in ōra vulgī? ([I don't know] *whether it is so that you might be on everyone's lips?*)

NEGATIVE ADVERBS (PARTICLES)

nōn (*not*), nē, in a prohibition (*not*)
haud (*not*), nē, in a purpose clause (*lest*)
minimē (*not at all*), nē, after verb of fearing (*that*)
nec, neque (*and not*), nēve, neu (*and not*)

neque . . . neque, nec . . . nec (*neither . . . nor*)
nē . . . quidem, with the emphasized word between (*not even*)
nōn sōlum . . . sed etiam (*not only . . . but also*)
nē quis, nē quid (*so that no one, so that nothing*)

RELATIVE ADVERBS

Relative adverbs introduce certain clauses:
> ubi (*where, when*) **ubi** iste post phasēlus anteā fuit comāta silva *where that future boat was previously a leafy forest*
> quō (*to where*) In arma feror **quō** tristis Erinys vocat. *I am borne into the arms to where the sad Fury calls.*
> unde (*from which place*) **unde** negant redīre quemquam *from where they say no one returns*
> cum (*when, since, although*) **cum** ausus es ūnus *when you alone dared*
>> (*why, therefore*) **quārē** habē tibi . . . *Therefore have for yourself . . .*

ADVERBS OF DEGREE

quam (*how*)
cūr, quārē (*why*)
ergō, itaque, igitur (*therefore*)
ita, sīc (*thus, so*)

paene (*almost*)
tam (*so*)
ut, utī (*how*)

Section 5: Verbs, Indicative and Imperative

Regular Verbs

In Latin the verb is especially important. It causes the subject either to act or to be acted upon. It expresses mood, voice, tense, person, and number. It includes four participles, the gerund, and the supine.

The present, imperfect, and the future indicative tenses, active and passive, are formed from the *present stem*, obtained by removing the -re from the present infinitive. The three perfect indicative active tenses are formed from the *perfect stem*, obtained by removing the -ī from the third principal part. The three perfect indicative passive tenses are formed from the fourth principal part, the entire *perfect passive participle*.

First Conjugation

PRINCIPAL PARTS OF PARŌ

parō	Pres. Ind., Act., 1st Sing.	*I prepare*
parāre	Pres. Inf. Act.	*to prepare*
parāvī	Perf. Ind. Act., 1st Sing.	*I have prepared, I prepared*
parātus	Perf. Pass. Part.	*having been prepared*

INDICATIVE ACTIVE

Present
parō *I prepare*
parās *you prepare*
parat *he prepares*
parāmus *we prepare*
parātis *you prepare*
parant *they prepare*

Perfect
parāvī *I have prepared*
parāvistī *you have prepared*
parāvit *he has prepared*
parāvimus *we have prepared*
parāvistis *you have prepared*
parāvērunt *they have prepared*

Imperfect
parābam *I was preparing*
parābās *you were preparing*
parābat *he was preparing*
parābāmus *we were preparing*
parābātis *you were preparing*
parābant *they were preparing*

Pluperfect
parāveram *I had prepared*
parāverās *you had prepared*
parāverat *he had prepared*
parāverāmus *we had prepared*
parāverātis *you had prepared*
parāverant *they had prepared*

Future
parābō *I shall prepare*
parābis *you will prepare*
parābit *he will prepare*
parābimus *we will prepare*
parābitis *you will prepare*
parābunt *they will prepare*

Future Perfect
parāverō *I shall have prepared*
parāveris *you will have prepared*
parāverit *he will have prepared*
parāverimus *we will have prepared*
parāveritis *you will have prepared*
parāverint *they will have prepared*

INDICATIVE PASSIVE

Present
paror *I am (being) prepared*
parāris *you are prepared*
parātur *he is prepared*
parāmur *we are prepared*
parāminī *you are prepared*
parantur *they are prepared*

Perfect
parātus, -a, -um **sum** *I have been prepared*
parātus, -a, -um **es** *you have been prepared*
parātus, -a, -um **est** *he has been prepared*
parātī, -ae, -a **sumus** *we have been prepared*
parātī, -ae, -a **estis** *you have been prepared*
parātī, -ae, -a **sunt** *they have been prepared*

Imperfect
parābar *I was being prepared*
parābāris *you were prepared*
parābātur *he was prepared*
parābāmur *we were prepared*
parābāminī *you were prepared*
parābantur *they were prepared*

Pluperfect
parātus, -a, -um **eram** *I had been prepared*
parātus, -a, -um **erās** *you had been prepared*
parātus, -a, -um **erat** *he had been prepared*
parātī, -ae, -a **erāmus** *we had been prepared*
parātī, -ae, -a **erātis** *you had been prepared*
parātī, -ae, -a **erant** *they had been prepared*

Future
parābor *I shall be prepared*
parāberis *you will be prepared*
parābitur *he will be prepared*
parābimur *we shall be prepared*
parābiminī *you will be prepared*
parābuntur *they will be prepared*

Future Perfect
parātus, -a, -um **erō** *I shall have been prepared*
parātus, -a, -um **eris** *you will have been prepared*
parātus, -a, -um **erit** *he will have been prepared*
parātī, -ae, -a **erimus** *we shall have been prepared*
parātī, -ae, -a **eritis** *you will have been prepared*
parātī, -ae, -a **erunt** *they will have been prepared*

IMPERATIVE ACTIVE
PRESENT
Sing.: parā — *prepare*
Plur.: parāte — *prepare*

IMPERATIVE PASSIVE
PRESENT
Sing.: parāre — *be prepared*
Plur.: parāminī — *be prepared*

SECOND CONJUGATION

PRINCIPAL PARTS OF HABEŌ
habeō *I have* **habēre** *to have* **habuī** *I have had* **habitus** *having been held*

INDICATIVE ACTIVE

Present	Perfect
habeō	habuī
habēs	habuistī
habet	habuit
habēmus	habuimus
habētis	habuistis
habent	habuērunt

Imperfect	Pluperfect
habēbam	habueram
habēbās	habuerās
habēbat	habuerat
habēbāmus	habuerāmus
habēbātis	habuerātis
habēbant	habuerant

Future	Future Perfect
habēbō	habuerō
habēbis	habueris
habēbit	habuerit
habēbimus	habuerimus
habēbitis	habueritis
habēbunt	habuerint

INDICATIVE PASSIVE

Present	Perfect
habeor	habitus, -a, -um **sum**
habēris	habitus, -a, -um **es**
habētur	habitus, -a, -um **est**
habēmur	habitī, -ae, -a **sumus**
habēminī	habitī, -ae, -a **estis**
habentur	habitī, -ae, -a **sunt**

Imperfect	Pluperfect
habēbar	habitus, -a, -um **eram**
habēbāris	habitus, -a, -um **erās**
habēbātur	habitus, -a, -um **erat**
habēbāmur	habitī, -ae, -a **erāmus**
habēbāminī	habitī, -ae, -a **erātis**
habēbantur	habitī, -ae, -a **erant**

Future	Future Perfect
habēbor	habitus, -a, -um **erō**
habēberis	habitus, -a, -um **eris**
habēbitur	habitus, -a, -um **erit**
habēbimur	habitī, -ae, -a **erimus**
habēbiminī	habitī, -ae, -a **eritis**
habēbuntur	habitī, -ae, -a **erunt**

IMPERATIVE ACTIVE
PRESENT
Sing.: habē
Plur.: habēte

IMPERATIVE PASSIVE
PRESENT
Sing.: habēre
Plur.: habēminī

THIRD CONJUGATION

PRINCIPAL PARTS OF DŪCŌ
dūcō *I lead* **dūcere** *to lead* **dūxī** *I have led* **ductus** *having been led*

The future active of the third conjugation is formed by adding -am, -ēs, -et, etc. to the present stem minus **-e**. To form the passive, -ar, -ēris, -ētur, etc. are added to the present stem minus **-e**.

INDICATIVE ACTIVE

Present	Perfect
dūcō	dūxī
dūcis	dūxistī
dūcit	dūxit
dūcimus	dūximus
dūcitis	dūxistis
dūcunt	dūxērunt

Imperfect	Pluperfect
dūcēbam	dūxeram
dūcēbās	dūxerās
dūcēbat	dūxerat
dūcēbāmus	dūxerāmus
dūcēbātis	dūxerātis
dūcēbant	dūxerant

Future	Future Perfect
dūcam	dūxerō
dūcēs	dūxeris
dūcet	dūxerit
dūcēmus	dūxerimus
dūcētis	dūxeritis
dūcent	dūxerint

INDICATIVE PASSIVE

Present	Perfect
dūcor	ductus, -a, -um **sum**
dūceris	ductus, -a, -um **es**
dūcitur	ductus, -a, -um **est**
dūcimur	ductī, -ae, -a **sumus**
dūciminī	ductī, -ae, -a **estis**
dūcuntur	ductī, -ae, -a **sunt**

Imperfect	Pluperfect
dūcēbar	ductus, -a, -um **eram**
dūcēbāris	ductus, -a, -um **erās**
dūcēbātur	ductus, -a, -um **erat**
dūcēbāmur	ductī, -ae, -a **erāmus**
dūcēbāminī	ductī, -ae, -a **erātis**
dūcēbantur	ductī, -ae, -a **erant**

Future	Future Perfect
dūcar	ductus, -a, -um **erō**
dūcēris	ductus, -a, -um **eris**
dūcētur	ductus, -a, -um **erit**
dūcēmur	ductī, -ae, -a **erimus**
dūcēminī	ductī, -ae, -a **eritis**
dūcentur	ductī, -ae, -a **erunt**

IMPERATIVE ACTIVE
Sing.: dūc[1]
Plur.: dūcite

IMPERATIVE PASSIVE
Sing.: dūcere
Plur.: dūciminī

[1]There are four verbs whose imperative omits the final "e" in the singular: dīc, dūc, fer, fac.

THE -IO VERBS OF THE 3RD CONJUGATION

PRINCIPAL PARTS OF CAPIŌ

capiō *I seize*   **capere** *to seize*   **cēpī** *I have seized*   **captus** *having been seized*

INDICATIVE

The six tenses of the indicative active are conjugated like audiō (4th conjugation) except that the -i of capiō is short throughout the present tense.

In the indicative passive, the second person singular, present passive, differs from its parallel in audiō: caperis, audīris.

IMPERATIVE ACTIVE	**IMPERATIVE PASSIVE**
Sing.: cape	*Sing.:* capere
Plur.: capite	*Plur.:* capiminī

FOURTH CONJUGATION

PRINCIPAL PARTS OF AUDIŌ

audiō *I hear*   **audīre** *to hear*   **audīvī** *I have heard*   **audītus** *having been heard*

INDICATIVE ACTIVE / INDICATIVE PASSIVE

INDICATIVE ACTIVE		**INDICATIVE PASSIVE**	
Present	*Perfect*	*Present*	*Perfect*
audiō	audīvī	audior	audītus, -a, -um **sum**
audīs	audīvistī	audīris	audītus, -a, -um **es**
audit	audīvit	audītur	audītus, -a, -um **est**
audīmus	audīvimus	audīmur	audītī, -ae, -a **sumus**
audītis	audīvistis	audīminī	audītī, -ae, -a **estis**
audiunt	audīvērunt	audiuntur	audītī, -ae, -a **sunt**
Imperfect	*Pluperfect*	*Imperfect*	*Pluperfect*
audiēbam	audīveram	audiēbar	audītus, -a, -um **eram**
audiēbās	audīverās	audiēbāris	audītus, -a, -um **erās**
audiēbat	audīverat	audiēbātur	audītus, -a, -um **erat**
audiēbāmus	audīverāmus	audiēbāmur	audītī, -ae, -a **erāmus**
audiēbātis	audīverātis	audiēbāminī	audītī, -ae, -a **erātis**
audiēbant	audīverant	audiēbantur	audītī, -ae, -a **erant**
Future	*Future Perfect*	*Future*	*Future Perfect*
audiam	audīverō	audiar	audītus, -a, -um **erō**
audiēs	audīveris	audiēris	audītus, -a, -um **eris**
audiet	audīverit	audiētur	audītus, -a, -um **erit**
audiēmus	audīverimus	audiēmur	audītī, -ae, -a **erimus**
audiētis	audīveritis	audiēminī	audītī, -ae, -a **eritis**
audient	audīverint	audientur	audītī, -ae, -a **erunt**

IMPERATIVE ACTIVE	**IMPERATIVE PASSIVE**
Sing.: audī	*Sing.:* audīre
Plur.: audīte	*Plur.:* audīminī

ALTERNATIVE AND SYNCOPATED VERB FORMS

Latin verbs have the following syncopated forms in poetry:

1. **Perfect active indicative, third person plural:** -ēre can be used instead of -ērunt in the perfect active indicative, third person plural. For example, **tenuēre** for **tenuērunt**. Be careful not to confuse such syncopated perfect endings with the endings of present infinitives in the second conjugation, i.e., **tenuēre** ("they held") and **tenēre** ("to hold").

2. **All verbs formed from the 3rd principal part:** The syllables –vi and –ve in the perfect tenses can be omitted. For example, **audierat** for **audīverat** and **amāsse** for **amāvisse**.

3. **Second person singular passive verbs that end in -ris.** The passive ending **-ris** is syncopated by using the ending -re instead. For example, **amābāre** for **amābāris** "you were loved."

INDICATIVE MOOD

1. The historical present is used in narratives about the past to make the past seem more vivid. It is not commonly used in love poetry. In other authors it looks like this: Mīlitēs iter **faciunt.** *The soldiers made a journey.*

2. **Iam** with any expression of time, plus the present, equals the English perfect: **Iam** Catullus diū Lesbiam **amat.** *Catullus has been loving Lesbia for a long time.* **Iam** plus the imperfect equals the English pluperfect: **Iam** Catullus multōs annōs Lesbiam **amābat.** *Catullus had now been loving Lesbia for many years.*

3. **Dum** *(while)* plus the present equals the English past. Dum Lesbia **adest,** Catullus laetus fuit. *While Lesbia was present, Catullus was happy.*

4. **Quamquam** and **etsī** *(although)* take any tense of the indicative: **quamquam** Lesbia non fidēlis **erat** *even though Lesbia was not faithful*

5. **Postquam** *(after)*, **ubi** *(when)*, **simul atque** *(as soon as)*, plus the Latin perfect, equal the English pluperfect: **postquam** Lesbia fūgit *after Lesbia had left*

6. Causal clauses introduced by **quod** or **quoniam** employ the indicative: **quod** Catullus Lesbiam amat *because Catullus loves Lesbia*

7. Temporal clauses introduced by **cum** and showing true time are in the indicative: **cum** vir adest *when her husband is present*

8. Relative clauses are usually in the indicative: unguentum **quod** meae puellae **dōnārunt** Venerēs Cupīdinēsque *the perfume which Venuses and Cupids gave my girl* (For relative clauses in the subjunctive, see below.)

DEPONENT VERBS (PASSIVE IN FORM; ACTIVE IN MEANING)

There are deponent verbs in all four conjugations. All are regularly passive in form. Exceptions are the future infinitive and the present and future participles, which are active in form.

THE IRREGULAR VERB SUM

PRINCIPAL PARTS
sum *I am*   **esse** *to be*   **fuī** *I have been*   **futūrus** *being about to be*

INDICATIVE

Present	Perfect	Imperfect	Pluperfect	Future	Future Perfect
sum	fuī	eram	fueram	erō	fuerō
es	fuistī	erās	fuerās	eris	fueris
est	fuit	erat	fuerat	erit	fuerit
sumus	fuimus	erāmus	fuerāmus	erimus	fuerimus
estis	fuistis	erātis	fuerātis	eritis	fueritis
sunt	fuērunt	erant	fuerant	erunt	fuerint

IMPERATIVE ACTIVE
Sing.: es   *be (you)*
Plur.: este   *be (you all)*

THE IRREGULAR VERB POSSUM

PRINCIPAL PARTS
possum *I am able*   **posse** *to be able*   **potuī** *I have been able*

INDICATIVE

Present	Perfect	Imperfect	Pluperfect	Future	Future Perfect
possum	potuī	poteram	potueram	poterō	potuerō
potes	potuistī	poterās	potuerās	poteris	potueris
potest	potuit	poterat	potuerat	poterit	potuerit
possumus	potuimus	poterāmus	potuerāmus	poterimus	potuerimus
potestis	potuistis	poterātis	potuerātis	poteritis	potueritis
possunt	potuērunt	poterant	potuerant	poterunt	potuerint

The Irregular Verb Ferō

PRINCIPAL PARTS
ferō *I bear*   **ferre** *to bear*   **tulī** *I have borne*   **lātus** *having been borne*

INDICATIVE ACTIVE

Present	Perfect	Imperfect	Pluperfect	Future	Future Perfect
ferō	tulī	ferēbam	tuleram	feram	tulerō
fers	tulistī	ferēbās	tulerās	ferēs	tuleris
fert	tulit	ferēbat	tulerat	feret	tulerit
ferimus	tulimus	etc.	etc.	etc.	etc.
fertis	tulistis				
ferunt	tulērunt				

INDICATIVE PASSIVE

Present	Perfect	Imperfect	Pluperfect	Future	Future Perfect
feror	lātus, -a, -um **sum**	ferēbar	lātus, -a, -um **eram**	ferar	lātus, -a, -um **erō**
ferris	lātus, -a, -um **es**	ferēbāris	lātus, -a, -um **erās**	ferēris	lātus, -a, -um **eris**
fertur	lātus, -a, -um **est**	ferēbātur	lātus, -a, -um **erat**	ferētur	lātus, -a, -um **erit**
ferimur	etc.	etc.	etc.	etc.	etc.
feriminī					
feruntur					

IMPERATIVE ACTIVE   **IMPERATIVE PASSIVE**
Sing.: fer   *Sing.:* ferre
Plur.: ferte   *Plur.:* feriminī

The Irregular Verb Eō[1]

PRINCIPAL PARTS
eō *I go*   **īre** *to go*   **iī (īvī)** *I have gone*   **itum (est)** *it has been gone*

INDICATIVE

Present	Perfect	Imperfect	Pluperfect	Future	Future Perfect
eō	iī	ībam	ieram	ībō	ierō
īs	iistī	ībās	ierās	ībis	ieris
it	iit	ībat	ierat	ībit	ierit
īmus	iimus	ībāmus	ierāmus	ībimus	ierimus
ītis	iistis	ībātis	ierātis	ībitis	ieritis
eunt	iērunt	ībant	ierant	ībunt	ierint

IMPERATIVE   **PARTICIPLES**
Present   *Present:* iēns (euntis)
Sing.: ī   *Future:* itūrus, -a, -um
Plur.: īte   *Gerundive:* eundus

[1]Adeō, ineō, and transeō are transitive and may therefore be conjugated in the passive. Queō and nequeō are conjugated like eō.

The Irregular Verbs Volō, Nōlō, and Mālō

Nōlō is made from nē-volō, while mālō is curtailed from magis-volō.
    Note: With the exception of the present tense, the forms of nōlō and mālō are similar to volō. For forms not given below, see volō, which is complete. Mālō and volō do not have imperative forms. Mālō is also deficient in participles.

PRINCIPAL PARTS
volō *I wish*   **velle** *to wish*   **voluī** *I have wished*

INDICATIVE

Present	Perfect	Imperfect	Pluperfect	Future	Future Perfect
volō	voluī	volēbam	volueram	volam	voluerō
vīs	voluistī	volēbās	voluerās	volēs	volueris
vult	voluit	volēbat	voluerat	volet	voluerit
volumus	voluimus	volēbāmus	voluerāmus	volēmus	voluerimus
vultis	voluistis	volēbātis	voluerātis	volētis	volueritis
volunt	voluērunt	volēbant	voluerant	volent	voluerint

PRINCIPAL PARTS
mālō *I prefer*   **mālle** *to prefer*   **māluī** *I have preferred*

INDICATIVE
Present
mālō
māvīs
māvult
mālumus
māvultis
mālunt

IMPERATIVE
(none)

PRINCIPAL PARTS
nōlō *I do not wish*   **nōlle** *to be unwilling*   **nōluī** *I have been unwilling*

INDICATIVE
Present
nōlō
nōn vīs
nōn vult
nōlumus
nōn vultis
nōlunt

IMPERATIVE[1]
Sing.: nōlī
Plur.: nōlīte

[1]These forms, plus a complementary infinitive, express a negative command.

THE IRREGULAR VERB FĪŌ

Note: Fīō is the irregular passive of faciō. Even though it is conjugated actively in the present, future, imperfect, it always has passive meaning.

PRINCIPAL PARTS
fīō *I am made*   **fierī** *to be made*   **factus** *having been made*

INDICATIVE

Present	Perfect	Imperfect	Pluperfect	Future	Future Perfect
fīō	factus, -a, -um **sum**	fīēbam	factus, -a, -um **eram**	fīam	factus, -a, -um **erō**
fīs	*etc.*	fīēbās	*etc.*	fīēs	*etc.*
fit		fīēbat		fīet	
fīmus		fīēbāmus		fīēmus	
fītis		fīēbātis		fīētis	
fīunt		fīēbant		fīent	

SECTION 6: INFINITIVES AND INDIRECT STATEMENT

FIRST CONJUGATION

INFINITIVES

ACTIVE
Present: parāre   *to prepare*
Perfect: parāvisse   *to have prepared*
Future: parātūrus esse   *to be about to prepare*

PASSIVE
Present: parārī   *to be prepared*
Perfect: parātus esse   *to have been prepared*
Future: parātum īrī (rare)   *to be about to be prepared*

SECOND CONJUGATION

INFINITIVES

ACTIVE
Present: habēre
Perfect: habuisse
Future: habitūrus esse

PASSIVE
Present: habērī
Perfect: habitus esse
Future: habitum īrī

THIRD CONJUGATION

INFINITIVES

ACTIVE		PASSIVE	
Pres.:	dūcere	*Pres.:*	dūcī[1]
Perf.:	dūxisse	*Perf.:*	ductus esse
Fut.:	ductūrus esse	*Fut.:*	ductum īrī

[1]To form the present passive infinitive, replace the -ere of the active form with -ī.

THIRD -IO CONJUGATION

INFINITIVES

ACTIVE		PASSIVE	
Pres.:	capere	*Pres.:*	capī
Perf.:	cēpisse	*Perf.:*	captus esse
Fut.:	captūrus esse	*Fut.:*	captum īrī

FOURTH CONJUGATION

INFINITIVES[2]

ACTIVE		PASSIVE	
Pres.:	audīre	*Pres.:*	audīrī
Perf.:	audīvisse	*Perf.:*	audītus esse
Fut.:	audītūrus esse	*Fut.:*	audītum īrī

[2]The present passive infinitive of the 1st, 2nd, and 4th conjugations is formed by replacing the final -e of the present active infinitive with an -ī.

IRREGULAR VERBS

Sum: **INFINITIVES**	Possum: **INFINITIVES**	Eō: **INFINITIVES**	Ferō: **INFINITIVES—ACTIVE**	**INFINITIVES—PASSIVE**
Pres.: esse	*Pres.:* posse	*Pres.:* īre	*Pres.:* ferre	*Pres.:* ferrī
Perf.: fuisse	*Perf.:* potuisse	*Perf.:* iisse	*Perf.:* tulisse	*Perf.:* lātus esse
Fut.: futūrus esse		*Fut.:* itūrus esse	*Fut.:* lātūrus esse	*Fut.:* lātum īrī

Volō: **INFINITIVES**	Nōlō: **INFINITIVES**	Mālō: **INFINITIVES**	Fīō: **INFINITIVES**
Pres.: velle	*Pres.:* nōlle	*Pres.:* mālle	*Pres.:* fierī
Perf.: voluisse	*Perf.:* nōluisse	*Perf.:* māluisse	*Perf.:* factus esse
		Fut.: factum īrī	

DEPONENT VERBS

Present:	farī	*to say*
Perfect:	fātus esse	*to have said*
Future:	fātūrus esse	*to be about to say*

SYNTAX OF THE INFINITIVE

1. In indirect statement when the statement made by a speaker is reported by someone, the subject is in the accusative case, the verb becomes an infinitive, and any subordinate verb becomes subjunctive. In deciding upon the tense of any subordinate verb, the sequence of tenses is followed. In deciding upon the tense of the infinitive, the problem may be resolved by returning the sentence to direct statement, and then using the same tense of the infinitive.

    Dīcit sē **venīre.** *He says that he is coming.* (direct: *I am coming.*)
    Dīxit sē **venīre.** *He said that he was coming.* (direct: *I am coming.*)
    Dīcit sē **vēnisse.** *He says that he has come.* (direct: *I have come.*)
    Dīxit sē **vēnisse.** *He said that he had come.* (direct: *I have come.*)
    Dīcit sē **ventūrum esse.** *He says that he will come.* (direct: *I shall come.*)
    Dīxit sē **ventūrum esse.** *He said that he would come.* (direct: *I shall come.*)

    Subordinate clauses occurring within an indirect statement are often conditions. In such cases, the "if clause" is in the subjunctive and the "conclusion" is an infinitive construction. Dīxit sī īret, nēminem secūtūrum **esse.** *He said that if he should go, no one should follow.*

2. Complementary Infinitive. An infinitive without a subject is used to complete the action of certain verbs:

    possum — *I am able*   statuō — *I determine*
    volō — *I wish*   cōnor — *I try*
    nōlō — *I do not wish*   temptō — *I try*
    mālō — *I prefer*   audeō — *I dare*
    cupiō — *I desire*   dēbeō — *I ought*
    patior — *I allow*   constituō — *I decide*
    dubitō — *I hesitate*   parō — *I prepare*
    incipiō — *I begin*   dēsistō — *I cease*
                                    videor — *I seem*

    nec **potis est** dulcīs Mūsārum **exprōmere** fētūs *and is not able to bring forth the sweet offspring of the Muses*

3. Objective Infinitive. Many verbs which ordinarily would take a complementary infinitive take an objective infinitive when the subject of the verb is different from the subject of the infinitive. Catullus Lesbiam iussit sibi mille bāsia **dare.** *Catullus asked Lesbia to give him a thousand kisses.*

4. Subjective Infinitive. Amāre bonum est. *It is good to be in love.*

5. Historical Infinitive. The infinitive, with a nominative subject, is sometimes used to express past time more vividly but this is not common in Catullus. Tum sīc **adfārī**. *Then she spoke thus.*

6. Exclamatory infinitive. This infinitive is used, with an accusative subject, as the main verb in the sentence, but this is not common in Catullus. mēne inceptō **dēsistere**? *that I desist from my undertaking?*

SECTION 7: PARTICIPLES

FIRST CONJUGATION

PARTICIPLES
Present Active: parāns, parantis — *preparing*
Perfect Passive: parātus, -a, -um — *(having been) prepared*
Future Active: parātūrus, -a, -um — *(being) about to prepare*

SECOND CONJUGATION

PARTICIPLES
Present Active: habēns, habentis — *having*
Perfect Passive: habitus, -a, -um — *(having been) held*
Future Active: habitūrus, -a, -um — *(being) about to hold*

THIRD CONJUGATION

PARTICIPLES
Present Active: dūcēns, dūcentis
Perfect Passive: ductus, -a, -um
Future Active: ductūrus, -a, -um

THIRD -IO CONJUGATION

PARTICIPLES
Present Active: capiēns, capientis
Perfect Passive: captus, -a, -um
Future Active: captūrus, -a, -um

FOURTH CONJUGATION

PARTICIPLES
Present Active: audiēns, audientis
Perfect Passive: audītus, -a, -um
Future Active: audītūrus, -a, -um

IRREGULAR VERBS

Sum:
PARTICIPLES
Fut.: futūrus, -a, -um

Possum:
PARTICIPLES
Pres.: potēns (*Gen.* potentis)

Eō:
PARTICIPLES
Pres.: iēns (euntis)
Fut.: itūrus, -a, -um
Gerundive: eundus

Ferō:
PARTICIPLES—ACTIVE
Pres.: ferēns
Fut.: lātūrus, -a, -um

PARTICIPLES—PASSIVE
Perf.: lātus, -a, -um
Ger.: ferendus, -a, -um

Volō:
PARTICIPLES
Pres.: volēns
(*Gen.:* volentis)

Nōlō:
PARTICIPLES
nōlēns
nōlentis (*Gen.*)

Fīō:
PARTICIPLES
Pres.: (none)
Perf.: factus
Gerundive: faciendus

DEPONENT VERBS

fāns — *saying* (1st conjug.)
fātus — *having said*
fātūrus — *being about to say*

SYNTAX OF PARTICIPLES

1. Participles are verbals which perform as adjectives. Lesbia, plurima mala **dīcēns** . . . *Lesbia, saying many bad things . . .*

2. The future active participle can express purpose. Fertur **moritūrus** in hostīs. *He is carried off against the enemy in order to die.*

3. Sometimes the present active participle can express purpose. Ībant **ōrantēs** veniam. *They went in order to pray for pardon.*

4. Participles are used with nouns and pronouns in the ablative case to express a subordinate clause indicating "when," "since," "although," etc. This construction is called an ablative absolute. Lesbia mī **praesente virō** mala plūrima dīcit. *With her husband present, Lesbia says many bad things to me.*

5. The future active participle combined with sum (first periphrastic conjugation) is a way of expressing futurity, even in past time. Lesbia plurima mala **dictūra erat.** *Lesbia was about to say many bad things.*

Section 8: Gerunds, Gerundives, and Supines

First Conjugation

GERUND

Nominative:	parāre	*preparing*
Genitive:	parandī	*of preparing*
Dative:	parandō	*for preparing*
Accusative:	parandum	*preparing*
Ablative:	parandō	*by preparing*

GERUNDIVE

parandus, -a, -um   *worthy to be prepared*

SUPINE

Acc.	parātum	*to prepare*
Abl.	parātū	*to prepare*

Second Conjugation

GERUND

Nom.:	habēre
Gen.:	habendī
Dat.:	habendō
Acc.:	habendum
Abl.:	habendō

GERUNDIVE

habendus, -a, -um

SUPINE

Acc.	habitum
Abl.	habitū

Third Conjugation

GERUND

Nom.:	dūcere
Gen.:	dūcendī
Dat.:	dūcendō
Acc.:	dūcendum
Abl.:	dūcendō

GERUNDIVE

dūcendus, -a, -um

SUPINE

Acc.	ductum
Abl.	ductū

Third -io Conjugation

GERUND

Nominative:	capere
Genitive:	capiendī
Dative:	capiendō
Accusative:	capiendum
Ablative:	cupiendō

GERUNDIVE

capiendus, -a, -um

SUPINE

Acc.	captum
Abl.	captū

Fourth Conjugation

GERUND

Nom.:	audīre
Gen.:	audiendī
Dat.:	audiendō
Acc.:	audiendum
Abl.:	audiendō

GERUNDIVE

audiendus, -a, -um

SUPINE

Acc.	audītum
Abl.	audītū

Irregular Verbs

Eō
GERUND

Nominative:	īre
Genitive:	eundī
Dative:	eundō
Accusative:	eundum
Ablative:	eundō

SUPINE

itum	*to go*
itū	*to go*

Ferō
GERUND

Nom.:	ferre
Gen.:	ferendī
Dat.:	ferendō
Acc.:	ferendum
Abl.:	ferendō

SUPINE

lātum
lātū

Syntax of Gerunds, Gerundives, and Supines

1. The gerund is a verbal noun which is declinable only in the singular. The gerund, as a verb, may take an object. **Voluptas vīvendī.** *Desire for living. Note:* There is no nominative form of the gerund. The subjective infinitive is used instead. (See Section 6.)

2. Future passive participles (sometimes called gerundives) express necessity or obligation. Dicta haud **dubitanda**. *Words by no means to be doubted.*

3. The future passive participle used with some form of sum is called the second periphrastic conjugation. Ūna nox perpetua **dormienda est**. *There is one perpetual night that must be slept.*

4. The accusative gerund or gerundive is used in Catullus to express purpose. Fabullus **ad cēnandum** vēnit. *Fabullus came (to Catullus' house) to eat dinner.*

5. The accusative supine (ending in **-um**) is used to express purpose with verbs of motion. Fabullus **cēnātum** vēnit. *Fabullus came to dine.*

6. The ablative supine (ending in **-ū**) is used with certain adjectives to indicate respect. Mīrābile **dictū**. *Marvelous to say.*

SECTION 9: SUBJUNCTIVE VERBS

No meanings are given for the subjunctive because of the great variety of its uses. Each use calls for its own, special translation.

FIRST CONJUGATION

SUBJUNCTIVE ACTIVE

Present	*Perfect*
parem	parāverim
parēs	parāverīs
paret	parāverit
parēmus	parāverīmus
parētis	parāverītus
parent	parāverint

Imperfect	*Pluperfect*
parārem	parāvissem
parārēs	parāvissēs
parāret	parāvisset
parārēmus	parāvissēmus
parārētis	parāvissētis
parārent	parāvissent

SUBJUNCTIVE PASSIVE

Present	*Perfect*
parer	parātus, -a, -um **sim**
parēris	parātus, -a, -um **sīs**
parētur	parātus, -a, -um **sit**
parēmur	parātī, -ae, -a **sīmus**
parēminī	parātī, -ae, -a **sītis**
parentur	parātī, -ae, -a **sint**

Imperfect	*Pluperfect*
parārer	parātus, -a, -um **essem**
parārēris	parātus, -a, -um **essēs**
parārētur	parātus, -a, -um **esset**
parārēmur	parātī, -ae, -a **essēmus**
parārēminī	parātī, -ae, -a **essētis**
parārentur	parātī, -ae, -a **essent**

SECOND CONJUGATION

SUBJUNCTIVE ACTIVE

Present	*Perfect*
habeam	habuerim
habeās	habuerīs
habeat	habuerit
habeāmus	habuerīmus
habeātis	habuerītis
habeant	habuerint

Imperfect	*Pluperfect*
habērem	habuissem
habērēs	habuissēs
habēret	habuisset
habērēmus	habuissēmus
habērētis	habuissētis
habērent	habuissent

SUBJUNCTIVE PASSIVE

Present	*Perfect*
habear	habitus, -a, -um **sim**
habeāris	habitus, -a, -um **sīs**
habeātur	habitus, -a, -um **sit**
habeāmur	habitī, -ae, -a **sīmus**
habeāminī	habitī, -ae, -a **sītis**
habeantur	habitī, -ae, -a **sint**

Imperfect	*Pluperfect*
habērer	habitus, -a, -um **essem**
habērēris	habitus, -a, -um **essēs**
habērētur	habitus, -a, -um **esset**
habērēmur	habitī, -ae, -a **essēmus**
habērēminī	habitī, -ae, -a **essētis**
habērentur	habitī, -ae, -a **essent**

THIRD CONJUGATION

SUBJUNCTIVE ACTIVE

Present	*Perfect*
dūcam	dūxerim
dūcās	dūxerīs
dūcat	dūxerit
dūcāmus	dūxerīmus
dūcātis	dūxerītis
dūcant	dūxerint

Imperfect	*Pluperfect*
dūcerem	dūxissem
dūcerēs	dūxissēs
dūceret	dūxisset
dūcerēmus	dūxissēmus
dūcerētis	dūxissētis
dūcerent	dūxissent

SUBJUNCTIVE PASSIVE

Present	*Perfect*
dūcar	ductus, -a, -um **sim**
dūcāris	ductus, -a, -um **sīs**
dūcātur	ductus, -a, -um **sit**
dūcāmur	ductī, -ae, -a **sīmus**
dūcāminī	ductī, -ae, -a **sītis**
dūcantur	ductī, -ae, -a **sint**

Imperfect	*Pluperfect*
dūcerer	ductus, -a, -um **essem**
dūcerēris	ductus, -a, -um **essēs**
dūcerētur	ductus, -a, -um **esset**
dūcerēmur	ductī, -ae, -a **essēmus**
dūcerēminī	ductī, -ae, -a **essētis**
dūcerentur	ductī, -ae, -a **essent**

THIRD -IO CONJUGATION

SUBJUNCTIVE

The imperfect subjunctive of capiō, both active and passive, is formed from the 2nd principal part capere, while audiō performs the same way. For example:

ACTIVE		**PASSIVE**	
caperem	audīrem	caperer	audīrer
etc.	*etc.*	*etc.*	*etc.*

Fourth Conjugation

SUBJUNCTIVE ACTIVE

Present	*Perfect*
audiam	audīverim
audiās	audīverīs
audiat	audīverit
audiāmus	audīverīmus
audiātis	audīverītis
audiant	audīverint

Imperfect	*Pluperfect*
audīrem	audīvissem
audīrēs	audīvissēs
audīret	audīvisset
audīrēmus	audīvissēmus
audīrētis	audīvissētis
audīrent	audīvissent

SUBJUNCTIVE PASSIVE

Present	*Perfect*
audiar	audītus, -a, -um **sim**
audiāris	audītus, -a, -um **sīs**
audiātur	audītus, -a, -um **sit**
audiāmur	audītī, -ae, -a **sīmus**
audiāminī	audītī, -ae, -a **sītis**
audiantur	audītī, -ae, -a **sint**

Imperfect	*Pluperfect*
audīrer	audītus, -a, -um **essem**
audīrēris	audītus, -a, -um **essēs**
audīrētur	audītus, -a, -um **esset**
audīrēmur	audītī, -ae, -a **essēmus**
audīrēminī	audītī, -ae, -a **essētis**
audīrentur	audītī, -ae, -a **essent**

Irregular Verbs

Sum
SUBJUNCTIVE

Present	*Perfect*
sim	fuerim
sīs	fuerīs
sit	fuerit
sīmus	fuerīmus
sītis	fuerītis
sint	fuerint

Imperf.	*Pluperf.*
essem	fuissem
essēs	fuissēs
esset	fuisset
essēmus	fuissēmus
essētis	fuissētis
essent	fuissent

Possum
SUBJUNCTIVE

Present	*Perfect*
possim	potuerim
possīs	potuerīs
possit	potuerit
possīmus	potuerīmus
possītis	potuerītis
possint	potuerint

Imperf.	*Pluperf.*
possem	potuissem
possēs	potuissēs
posset	potuisset
possēmus	potuissēmus
possētis	potuissētis
possent	potuissent

Eō
SUBJUNCTIVE

Present	*Perfect*
eam	ierim
eās	ierīs
eat	ierit
eāmus	ierīmus
eātis	ierītis
eant	ierint

Imperf.	*Pluperf.*
īrem	iissem (īssem)
īrēs	iissēs
īret	iisset
īrēmus	iissēmus
īrētis	iissētis
īrent	iissent

Volō
SUBJUNCTIVE

Present	*Perfect*
velim	voluerim
velīs	voluerīs
velit	voluerit
velīmus	voluerīmus
velītis	voluerītis
velint	voluerint

Imperfect	*Pluperfect*
vellem	voluissem
vellēs	voluissēs
vellet	voluisset
vellēmus	voluissēmus
vellētis	voluissētis
vellent	voluissent

Ferō
SUBJUNCTIVE ACTIVE

Present	*Perfect*
feram	tulerim
ferās	tulerīs
ferat	tulerit
etc.	etc.

Imperf.	*Pluperf.*
ferrem	tulissem
ferrēs	tulissēs
ferret	tulisset
etc.	etc.

SUBJUNCTIVE PASSIVE

Present	*Perfect*
ferar	lātus, -a, -um **sim**
ferāris	lātus, -a, -um **sīs**
ferātur	lātus, -a, -um **sit**
etc.	etc.

Imperf.	*Pluperfect*
ferrer	lātus, -a, -um **essem**
ferrēris	lātus, -a, -um **essēs**
ferrētur	lātus, -a, -um **esset**
etc.	etc.

Nōlō
SUBJUNCTIVE

Present
nōlim
nōlīs
nōlit
nōlīmus
nōlītis
nōlint

Mālō
SUBJUNCTIVE

Present
mālim
mālīs
mālit
mālīmus
mālītis
mālint

Fīō
SUBJUNCTIVE

Present	*Perfect*	*Imperfect*	*Pluperfect*
fīam	factus, -a, -um **sim**	fierem	factus, -a, -um **essem**
fīās	etc.	fierēs	etc.
fīat		fieret	
fīāmus		fierēmus	
fīātis		fierētis	
fīant		fierent	

Most compounds of faciō become -ficiō, while factus becomes -fectus. They are conjugated like capiō. *But* the passive of satisfaciō is satisfīō.

Subjunctive Mood—Independent Uses

1. **The volitive subjunctive**: The volitive subjunctive (sometimes called hortatory and sometimes jussive) indicates a weak command or encouragement. In the first and third persons, singular and plural, the volitive subjunctive is translated into English with the word "let." In the second person singular and plural, the English word "may" is used.

    Vīvāmus, mea Lesbia, atque **amēmus**.   *Let's live, my Lesbia, and let's love.*

    Dēsinās ineptīre.   *May you stop being a fool.*

2. **The optative subjunctive**: The optative subjunctive is a sentence which expresses a wish. The present subjunctive translates with the word "may."

    Hic libellum **maneat** plūs ūnō perenne saeclō.   *May this book last more than one age.*

3. **The deliberative subjunctive**: The deliberative subjunctive is a question in which something is being considered or deliberated. The present subjunctive is translated into English with phrases like "Am I to . . . ?", "Are you to . . . ?", etc.

    Hoc quid **putēmus** esse?   *What are we to make of this?*

4. **The potential subjunctive**: The potential subjunctive is a sentence which expresses the opinion of the speaker as an opinion. The present subjunctive translates with "should, would" or in potential questions with "can."

    nec bāsia pernumerāre cūriōsī **possint**   *and the busy-bodies would not be able to count the kisses*

Subjunctive Mood—Dependent Uses

1. Any subordinate clause introduced by an interrogative word is an indirect question. It ordinarily depends upon a verb of *knowing, telling, seeing, hearing,* or any expression of uncertainty. The verb of the indirect question goes in the subjunctive. The tense of the subjunctive clause depends upon whether the action of the indicative verb in the main clause is continuing or complete. There are two sequences of tenses (depending upon the two possible times of the main verb):

    A. **Primary** (main verb in present time):

    Scit quid **faciam.** *He knows what I am doing.*

    Scit quid **factūrus sim.**[1] *He knows what I shall do.*

    Scit quid **fēcerim.** *He knows what I did.*

    B. **Secondary** (main verb in past time):

    Scīvit quid **facerem.** *He knew what I was doing.*

    Scīvit quid **factūrus essem.**[1] *He knew what I was going to do.*

    Scīvit quid **fēcissem.** *He knew what I had done.*

2. Purpose Clauses — Adverbial. The purpose clause, usually introduced by ut or nē, modifies the verb. Pos.: Catullus Rōmam vēnit **ut** Lesbiam vidēret. *Catullus came to Rome to see Lesbia.* Neg.: Conturbābimus illa bāsia, **nē sciāmus** . . . *We will mix up the number of those kisses so that even we might not know . . .*

3. Purpose Clauses — Relative. The purpose clause, introduced by a relative pronoun or adjective, is adjectival. Tibī poēma fēcī, **ex quō perspicerēs** meum dolōrem. *I made this poem for you so that from it you might see my sorrow.*

4. Purpose Clauses — Substantive. The clause, usually introduced by ut or nē, is the object of a verb of urging, allowing, willing, desiring, etc. Deōs rogābis tōtum **ut tē faciant,** Fabulle, nāsum. *You will ask the gods to make you all nose, Fabullus.*

5. Result Clauses — Adverbial. Result clauses generally follow a "so" word such as tam or tantum. The negative is not ne but ut + a negative word. Pos.: Catullus **tam** Lesbiam amat **ut** miser **sit.** *Catullus loves Lesbia so much that he is miserable.* Neg: **Tam** incēnsus, eram, **ut nec** mē cibus **iuvāret neque** somnus **tegeret** ocellōs. *I was so worked up that food did not help me and sleep did not cover my eyes.*

6. Result Clauses — Substantive. Accidit **ut** Catullus Lesbiam **amet.** *It happens that Catullus loves Lesbia.*

7. After verbs of fearing. Pos.: Catullus verētur **nē** Lesbia alium **amet.** *Catullus is afraid that Lesbia loves someone else.* Neg.: Catullus verētur **ut** Lesbia sē **amet.** *Catullus is afraid that Lesbia does not love him.*

8. **Cum** Clauses (when **cum** means *when, since,* or *although*). **Cum** Catullus Lesbiam **videat,** laetus est. *When Catullus sees Lesbia he is happy.*

9. After **dum** (meaning *until*). Catullus Lesbiam petīvit **dum** eam **invenīret.** *Catullus looked for Lesbia until he found her.* (Anticipatory subjunctive: "until he might find her.")

10. Expressions of doubt and hindering, generally with the word quīn. Nōn dubium est **quīn** Catullus Lesbiam **amet.** *There is no doubt that Catullus loves Lesbia.*

11. Relative Clause of Description. Amor **quī** virōs vēsanōs **faciat.** *The kind of love that makes men crazy.*

[1]Since in this instance a future form of the subjunctive is needed, the present and imperfect forms of the verb **sum** are used, along with the future participle, to take the place of the missing form.

SECTION 10: CONDITIONS

SIMPLE CONDITIONS

1. Present: present indicative tense

    Sī Lesbia laeta **est,** Catullus laetus **est.**
    If Lesbia is happy, then Catullus is happy.

2. Past: past indicative tense

    Sī Lesbia laeta **erat,** Catullus laetus **erat.**
    If Lesbia was happy, then Catullus was happy.

FUTURE VIVID CONDITIONS

3. Future More Vivid: future perfect and future tenses

    Sī Lesbia laeta **fuerit,** Catullus laetus **erit.**
    If Lesbia will be happy, then Catullus will be happy.

4. Future Less Vivid: present subjunctive tense

    Sī Lesbia laeta **sit,** Catullus laetus **sit.**
    If Lesbia should (happen to be) happy, then Catullus would be happy.

CONTRARY-TO-FACT CONDITIONS

5. Present: imperfect subjunctive tense

    Sī Lesbia laeta **esset,** Catullus laetus **esset.**
    If Lesbia were happy, then Catullus would be happy.

6. Past: pluperfect subjunctive tense

    Sī Lesbia laeta **fuisset,** Catullus laetus **fuisset.**
    If Lesbia had been happy, then Catullus would have been happy.

SECTION 11: VOICE

The voice of a verb indicates whether the subject is acting (active voice) or being acted upon (passive voice). Greek has a third voice (middle) used to indicate that the subject is acting upon itself. English and Latin usually express the middle voice by the use of reflexive pronouns. Vergil sometimes uses passive verb forms as a middle/reflexive. Passive verbs do not normally take a direct object. A Latin verb in the passive voice **with** a direct object is usually being used as a reflexive/ middle voice verb.

Sinūs **collēcta** (est) fluentēs. *She gathered (for herself) the flowing folds (of her garments).*

SECTION 12: INFORMATION ON METER

QUANTITY

The quantity of a syllable is the term used to denote the relative amount of time employed in pronouncing it. About twice as much time should be used in pronouncing a long syllable as a short one.

A syllable is said to be long by *nature,* when it contains a long vowel or a diphthong. It is said to be long by *position* when its vowel is followed by two or more consonants which are separated in pronunciation, or by either of the double consonants **x** or **z,** or by **j,** which was regularly doubled in pronunciation. **H** never helps to make a syllable long, and **qu** counts as a single consonant. Thus the first syllable of **adhūc,** *thus far,* and of **aqua,** *water,* is short.

Except under the metrical accent, a final syllable ending in a short vowel regularly remains short before a word beginning with two consonants or a double consonant.

If a consonant followed by **l** or **r** comes after a short vowel, the syllable containing the short vowel is said to be *common,* i.e., it may be either long or short, according to the pleasure of the one using it.

Note: This is due to the fact that the **l** and **r** blend so easily with the preceding consonant that the combination takes scarcely more time than a single consonant. When the l or r is separated in pronunciation from the preceding consonant, as may be done in all cases, more time is required in pronunciation and the preceding syllable is treated as long.

Observe that the *vowel* in a long syllable may be either long or short, and is to be pronounced accordingly. Thus in **errō,** *wander;* **captō,** *seize;* **vertō,** *turn;* **nox,** *night;* the first *vowel* in each case is short, and must be so pronounced, but the syllable is long, and must occupy more time in pronunciation.

A vowel is regularly short before another vowel, or **h,** as **aes-tu-ō,** *boil;* **de-us,** *god;* **tra-hō,** *draw.*
    a. This rule does not apply to Greek words in Latin, such as **a-er,** *air;* **I-xī-ōn,** *Ixion* (a proper name).

A vowel is regularly short before **nt** or **nd.** Observe that the *syllable* is this case is long.

A vowel is regularly short before any final consonant except **s.**
    a. Some monosyllables ending in **l, r, n,** and **c,** have a long vowel as **sōl,** *sun;* **pār,** *equal;* **nōn,** *not;* **sīc,** *so.*

A vowel is regularly long before **ns, nf, nx,** and **nct.**

Diphthongs and vowels derived from diphthongs or contracted from other vowels are regularly long.

VERSIFICATION

THE DACTYLIC HEXAMETER

One of the most common meters of Latin poetry is the **dactylic hexameter**. It was commonly employed by the Greeks and Romans in epic (narrative) poetry, such as the *Iliad* and the *Odyssey* of Homer, the *Aeneid* of Vergil, and the *Metamorphoses* of Ovid. It is occasionally used in English, as in Longfellow's *Evangeline*. Some of the most beautiful Latin hexameters ever written are those of Vergil and Ovid.

There are six feet in a hexameter (Gr. **hex,** *six;* **metron,** *measure*) verse or line. The first five feet are either dactyls (Gr. **dactylos,** *finger*), i.e., one long syllable followed by two shorts (— ∪ ∪), or spondees, i.e., two longs (— —). The sixth foot is always treated as a spondee (— —).

The final syllable of a hexameter verse may be either long or short (**syllaba anceps**); but for practical purposes in scansion it may be considered long and thus marked.

The Metrical Scheme of a verse is thus:

$$ — \acute{}\ \cup\cup\ \ —\ \acute{}\ \cup\cup\ \ —\ \acute{}\ \cup\cup\ \ —\ \acute{}\ \cup\cup\ \ —\ \acute{}\ \cup\cup\ \ —\ \acute{}\ \cup $$

i.e., the first syllable of each foot must be long. It is also given slightly more stress than the other half of the foot. This stress is called the metrical accent.

    a. A short syllable is often lengthened under the metrical accent or before a pause.

The fifth foot of the hexameter is almost always a dactyl. When a spondee is used in this place, it gives the verse a slower movement then usual. Such a verse is then called spondaic.

For metrical purposes each syllable of a Latin verse is considered either long or short, a long syllable occupying approximately twice as much time as short. For this reason a spondaic foot (— —) is considered the metrical equivalent of a dactylic foot. (— ∪ ∪).

Observe that only vowels long by nature are marked in the Latin words in this book.

Elision. Whenever a word ends with a vowel, diphthong, or **m,** and the following words begin with a vowel or **h,** the first vowel or diphthong is regularly elided. Elision is not a total omission, but rather a light and hurried half-pronunciation, somewhat similar to grace notes in music.

Hiatus. Occasionally a word ending in a vowel, diphthong, or m is followed by a word beginning with a vowel or **h** and elision does not take place. This is called hiatus.

Semi-hiatus. Sometimes when a word ends in a long vowel or a diphthong and the next word begins with a vowel or **h,** the long final vowel or diphthong is shortened. This is called semi-hiatus.

The vowels **i** and **u** are sometimes used as consonants (**j, v**), as **abiete** (pronounce **abjete**), **genua** (pronounce **genva**).

Hypermeter. Sometimes the final syllable at the end of a verse is elided before a vowel at the beginning of the following verse. This is called synapheia, and the verse whose final syllable is elided is called a hypermeter or a hypermetric verse.

Synizesis. Two successive vowels which do not ordinarily form a diphthong are sometimes pronounced as one syllable for the sake of the meter. This sort of contraction of two syllables into one within a word is called synizesis.

SCANSION

Observe the scansion of the following passage:

Arma virumque canō, Troiae quī prīmus ab ōrīs

Ītaliam fātō profugus Lāvīnaque vēnit

lītora, multum ille et terrīs iactātus et altō

vī superum saevae memorem Iūnōnis ob īram,

multa quoque et bellō passus, dum conderet urbem

īnferretque deōs Latiō; genus unde Latīnum

Albānīque patrēs atque altae moenia Rōmae.

In marking the scansion the sign (—) is used to indicate a long *syllable* and the sign (∪) for a short *syllable*. The feet are separated from each other by the perpendicular line (|), the metrical accent is indicated by a (´) over the first syllable of each foot, and elision is indicated by a (‿) connecting the elided vowel with the vowel following.

Hints on the Metrical Reading of Latin Poetry

In reading Latin poetry orally, the words should be kept distinct and no break made between the separate feet, unless there is a pause in sense.

Careful attention should be paid to the meaning of the passage, and the various pauses in sense should be indicated by the voice. Of course the voice should not be allowed to drop at the end of a verse unless there is a distinct pause in sense.

Remember that the rhythm of Latin verse is based primarily upon the regular succession of long and short syllables, that of English primarily on the succession of accented and unaccented syllables.

To obtain facility in reading Latin verse, a considerable amount of it should be memorized, special attention being paid to the quantity, i.e., approximately twice as much time should be given to each long syllable as to a short one.

Caesúra. Whenever a word ends within a foot the break is called caesura. If this coincides with a pause in the verse, it is called the principal caesura, or sometimes simply the caesura of the verse.

A single verse may have more than one caesura, each marked by a pause in sense. The principal caesuras are: (1) After the first long syllable of the third foot; (2) After the first long syllable of the fourth foot.

APPENDIX B

MAJOR FIGURES OF SPEECH FOUND IN THIS BOOK

Alliterátion is the repetition of the same letter or sound, as the sound of *m* in **ut tē postrēmō dōnārem mūnere mortis,** *that I might present you with death's final offering.*

Anáphora is the repetition of a word or words at the beginning of successive clauses, as **quae Syrtis, quae Scylla rapax, quae vasta Charybdis,** *what Syrtis, what ravenous Scylla, what bottomless Charybdis (gave birth to you)?*

Anástrophe is an inversion of the usual order of words, as **tē propter,** *on account of you.*

Antíthesis is an opposition or contrast of words or ideas, as **nōs aliō mentēs, aliō dīvīsimus aurēs** *we have divided our minds one way, our ears another*

Apóstrophe is a sudden break from the previous method of discourse and an addressing, in the second person, of some person or object, absent or present, as **Salvē, ō venuste Sirmiō, atque erō gaudē gaudente** *Hail, o charming Sirmio, and rejoice with your rejoicing master.* Here Catullus addresses his villa at Sirmio.

Asýndeton is the omission of conjunctions, as **mihi candida longa recta est,** *to me she is fair, tall, upright.*

Brachýlogy (breviloquéntia) is the failure to repeat an element that is to be supplied in a more or less modified form, as **tam fēlīx essēs quam formōsissima (es) vellem,** *would that you were as fortunate as (you are) fair.* What we call "gapping" in this book can be often be considered a type of brachylogy.

Chiásmus is the arrangement of corresponding pairs of words in opposite order, as <u>formōsa</u> est *multīs, mihi* <u>candida,</u> *she is beautiful to many, to me fair.*

Eúphony is the effect produced by words or sounds so combined and uttered as to please the ear.

Hendíadys is the expression of an idea by means of two nouns connected by a conjunction instead of by a noun and a limiting adjective as in **in iocō atque vīnō,** "in joke and wine" meaning "in drunken play."

Hypérbaton or **Trajéction** is the violent displacement of words, **aurātam optantēs Colchīs āvertere pellem,** *desiring to turn the golden fleece away from the Colchians.*

Hypérbole is rhetorical exaggeration, as **quōs simul complexa tenet trecentōs** *three hundred of whom she holds in her embrace at the same time.*

Irony is a sort of humor, ridicule, or light sarcasm that states an apparent fact with the clear intention of expressing its opposite. Often in Catullus, the irony is only clear later on in the poem. Thus, in poem 13, **Cēnābis bene,** *you will dine well,* is actually ironic, but this is only clear as you read further.

Lítotes or **Understatement** is the use of an expression by which more is meant than meets the ear. This is especially common with the negative as **Salvē, nec minimō puella nāsō,** *Greetings, girl with a not too small nose.*

Métaphor is an implied comparison, as **lectī iuvenēs, rōbora Argīvae pubis,** *chosen young men, the oaks of Argive youth.*

Metónymy is the substitution of one word for another that it suggests, as **gemina teguntur lūmina nocte,** *their eyes (lights) are covered by twin night.*

Onomatopoéia is the use of words of which the sound suggests the sense, as **tintinant aurēs,** *my ears ring.*

Oxymóron is the use of words apparently contradictory of each other, as **ōdī et amō,** *I hate and I love.*

Personification is an attribution of the element of personality to an impersonal thing, **pīnūs dīcuntur liquidās Neptūnī nāsse per undās,** *the pines are said to have swum through Neptune's liquid waves.*

Polysýndeton is the use of unnecessary conjunctions, as **et vīnō et sale et omnibus cachinnīs,** *and wine and wit and all manner of laughter.*

Símile is a figure of speech that likens or asserts an explicit comparison between two different things in one or more of their aspects, as when Catullus compares his crushed hopes and tender love to a flower that is killed by a plow: **velut prātī ultimī flōs,** *like a flower at the edge of a meadow.*

Sýnchesis is an interlocked order of words, **as *caerula* verrentēs <u>abiegnīs</u> *aequora* <u>palmīs</u>,** *sweeping the blue waters with pine blades.*

Synécdoche is the use of a part for the whole, or the reverse, as **ausī sunt vada salsa cita dēcurrere puppī,** *they dared to speed through the salty sea on a swift stern* (where "stern" = "ship").

A Transferred Epithet is an epithet that has been transferred from the word to which it strictly belongs to another word connected with it in thought, as **manat tristī cōnscius ōre rubor,** *a knowing blush flows over her sad face.*

Tricolon is the use of three parallel clauses or phrases occurring together in a series, as **quīcum lūdere, quem in sinū tenēre, cui prīmum digitum dare,** *with whom (she was accustomed) to play, whom (she was accustomed) to hold in her bosom, to whom (she was accustomed) to give her finger tip.* In this case, since each clause is longer than the one before it, it is called **tricolon crescens**.

OTHER TRANSITIONAL READERS

The *LEGAMUS Transitional Readers* and *Little Book of Latin Love Poetry* are innovative texts that form a bridge between the initial study of Latin via basal textbooks and the reading of authentic author texts. This series of texts is being developed by a special committee of high school and college teachers to facilitate this challenging transition.

- This series of texts was developed by a special committee of high school and college teachers to facilitate this challenging transition.
- Each transitional reader has approximately 200 lines of Latin accompanied by: pre-reading materials ▪ grammatical exercises ▪ complete vocabulary ▪ notes designed for reading comprehension ▪ other reading aids.
- Introductory materials and illustrations are included. Appendices (on grammar, figures of speech, and meter where appropriate) and a pull-out vocabulary complete these books' innovative features.
- After finishing a transitional reader, students will be prepared to undertake a more complete study of the author as a college or advanced high school author course.

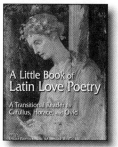

VERGIL: A LEGAMUS Transitional Reader
Thomas J. Sienkewicz and LeaAnn A. Osburn

This reader contains selections 227 lines from Vergil's *Aeneid*, Books I, II, and IV.

Student Text: xxiv + 135 pp. (2004) 8½" x 11" Paperback, ISBN 978-0-86516-578-6
Teacher's Guide: x + 72 pp. (2010) 6" x 9" Paperback, ISBN 978-0-86516-579-3

OVID: A LEGAMUS Transitional Reader
Caroline Perkins and Denise Davis-Henry

This reader contains 202 lines of Latin selections from Ovid poems.

Student Text: xxvi + 127 pp (2007) 8½" x 11" Paperback, ISBN 978-0-86516-604-2
Teacher's Guide: vii + 51 pp. (2010) 6" x 9" Paperback, ISBN 978-0-86516-734-6

HORACE: A LEGAMUS Transitional Reader
Ronnie Ancona and David J. Murphy

This reader contains 202 lines of Latin selections from Horace's *Odes* and *Satires*.

Student Text: xxiv + 189 pp (2008) 8½" x 11" Paperback, ISBN 978-0-86516-676-9
Teacher's Guide: viii + 76 pp. (2010) 6" x 9" Paperback, ISBN 978-0-86516-732-2

CICERO: A LEGAMUS Transitional Reader
Judith Sebesta and Mark Haynes

This reader features 103 lines from the *Pro Archia*.

Student Text: xxi + 222 pp. (2010) 8½" x 11" Paperback, ISBN 978-0-86516-656-1
Teacher's Guide: x + 68 pp. (2010) 6" x 9" Paperback, ISBN 978-0-86516-735-3

CAESAR: A LEGAMUS Transitional Reader
Rose Williams and Hans-Friedrich Mueller

This reader features 325 lines from the *De Bello Gallico* and the *De Bello Civili*.

Student Text: xviii + 287 pp. (2012) 8½" x 11" Paperback, ISBN 978-0-86516-733-9
Teacher's Guide: xii + 169 pp. (2012) 6" x 9" Paperback, ISBN 978-0-86516-736-0

A Little Book of Latin Love Poetry
A Transitional Reader for Catullus, Horace, and Ovid
John Breuker and Mardah B. C. Weinfeld

Student Text: xii + 138 pp. (2006) 8 ½" x 11" Paperback, ISBN 978-0-86516-601-1
Teacher's Guide: xii + 155 pp. (2006) 8 ½" x 11" Paperback, ISBN 978-0-86516-636-3

Love Poetry Readings for Comprehension and Review
Selections (**156 lines**) from 6 poems of Catullus (51, 43, 86, 5, 70, 8), 3 poems of Horace (I.23, III.9, III.26), and 2 poems of Ovid (Amores 1.5 and 1.9), first modified, then unmodified ▪ Opposite-page Vocabulary and Reading Helps, and Questions on Analysis/Comprehension, and on Literary Analysis/Discussion ▪ 13 Rapid Reviews of grammar/syntax with exercises ▪ 2 Major Reviews with drills ▪ Final Unit Review with all poems in unmodified form with notes on Textual Matters and Points to Ponder ▪ 4 Appendices: Timeline; Poetic Devices/Literary Terms; Metrics; Grammar and Syntax ▪ Bibliography ▪ Glossary of Proper Names ▪ Full Latin-English Vocabulary

BOLCHAZY-CARDUCCI PUBLISHERS, INC.
WWW.BOLCHAZY.COM

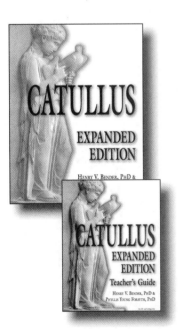